End

It took a unique vision for Chris Galanos to launch a non-traditional, cell church strategy after completing his seminary degree. But it took much more courage for him to ask 12 people to engage a vision of a church reaching 10,000 in 10 years. But when that happened in less than 9 years, the Holy Spirit invited Chris to engage in a truly paradigm-busting vision.

For this task, most conventions of traditional ministry would have to be jettisoned in order to see 1,000,000 lost people become obedient disciples of Jesus. And after a season of preparation for that goal, the day came when Chris and his ministry team asked thousands of people to consider being trained and coached to depart the church to make disciples and plant simple replicating churches.

This book is a very candid and winsome telling of Chris's and his team's journey toward that vision, and how insights from Kingdom Movements around the world have shaped the process. This book is easy to read, but it is not for the faint of heart. It will elevate your vision, animate your prayers, and invite you to find what "exceedingly, beyond what you can think or imagine" means for you.

JERRY TROUSDALE
Author of *Miraculous Movements*
and Co-Author of *The Kingdom Unleashed*
Director of International Ministries
New Generations

I have known Chris Galanos since 1998. His mother served on the board of Asian Partners International, the mission agency I founded, and his father met with me and others every Tuesday morning for several years to pray for Asian Partners and their ministries. It has been fun to watch Chris as he started his church and it grew beyond all expectations. I have had several opportunities to visit with Chris over the past ten years, and one thing sticks out: Chris wants to be on the front line of wherever God is at work. Chris's new book is the story of "What's next?" for an incredibly successful megachurch pastor when the megachurch he founded was not capable of reaching all peoples in all nations. His book tells of the struggles within his core staff, as well as with his church members, as he continues to explore where the front line of God's work is for him and his team. The book is an easy read and will challenge anyone who reads it to ask the question, "What's it going to take to fulfill the Great Commission in our generation?"

DAVID WATSON

Co-Author of *Contagious Disciple Making:*
Leading Others on a Journey of Discovery

Very few men have dared to ask the God-sized questions that it takes to change the world; and once they get the answer, then dare to take the *giant* steps of faith required of a leader to achieve the *big*, God-sized vision. Nehemiah is remembered as a great leader who dared to ask, "What's it gonna take?" to build a wall around Jerusalem. Moses is remembered as a great leader who dared to ask, "What's it gonna take?" to lead the Israelites out of slavery in Egypt. Joshua is remembered as a great leader who dared to ask, "What's it gonna take?" to claim the promised land. Solomon is remembered as a great leader who dared to ask, "What's it gonna take?" to build the Temple.

For these ordinary men who dared to ask the big questions, God granted them wisdom, courage, and an extra measure of faith to do what seemed to their generation as the impossible. Chris Galanos is a twenty-first-century version of these men. He is a man of tremendous faith and courage with an unusual amount of boldness and wisdom who has dared to ask the big question, "What's it gonna take?" to reach the people groups of the melting pot called the United States of America.

Over our brief two hundred–plus years of history as a nation, has anyone dared to ask the question and then purposed in his or her heart to make the necessary sacrifices needed to reach our nation with the gospel? Having known Chris and watched his journey of faith, I am confident that his God-sized vision to reach our nation with the gospel is neither a pipe dream nor a delusion of grandeur. He is a man of God who hears from God and strives to walk in obedience to what God has put on his heart. I challenge the reader to watch the hand of God as he uses his vessel to accomplish his purposes. However, we must not just watch but pray for wisdom for Chris and his team and for God's protection from the evil one. This man of God with a God-sized vision is a threat to the kingdom of darkness. May God bring to pass what he has put in Chris's heart, and may a true Disciple Making Movement sweep the land.

Our nation desperately needs a Third Great Awakening. All of us who will take the time to read Chris's book must not be just passive readers but earnestly ask, "Lord, what is my part in this vision?" The marching orders of the Great Commission are not just for Chris and his team; they are for all of us who claim to be Christ followers. May this book spur us on to make disciples who become disciple makers.

DR. SAM DOUGLASS
Director of Reaching Unreached and Unengaged People
Groups for Dynamic Church Planting International

One million souls in ten years sounds too big and impossible, but knowing the Lord of the harvest personally, nothing is too big or impossible for him.

I have known Chris Galanos for the past twelve years. His incessant love and ever-increasing faith in the Lord Jesus Christ are well known. I have always admired his commitment and obedience to the Great Commission of our Lord. Applying the Great Commission in one's life and ministry is joining the unstoppable movement of God.

The Gospel Movement leads to Disciple Making Movements, which will bring an increase of disciples who then will become harvesters and leaders in the reshaped movement of God for this generation. This increase should push more laborers to future unreached areas to make new disciples who will be gathered into churches and who will then begin to make more disciples.

It is an honor to recommend this publication for Chris Galanos and rejoice in things yet to come.

VICTOR JOHN
President (ASSI)
VP Global CPM (APII)

If there has ever been a time for a voice in America to beckon believers to multiply the church and complete the Great Commission, the time is now and Pastor Chris is one of those dear voices. I know Pastor Chris to unashamedly proclaim the good news of Jesus Christ and prepare new believers to stand together with the persecuted church.

BROTHER YUN
The Heavenly Man
Chinese Underground Church Leader
Back to Jerusalem

Chris Galanos is not just a world-class visionary leader, he is a man of God. The principles in this book will most certainly lead to significant Kingdom impact if applied consistently and effectively. Chris is a master disciple maker and has a miraculous testimony in seeing the power of God change an entire city!

JOEL ENGLE
Pastor of Preaching & Vision
ChangePoint Church
Anchorage, Alaska

There has been explosive growth of new disciples and churches in much of the developing world for some decades now. Some pastors like Chris Galanos see that and ask, "Why not in my city? What will it take to restore my people group to full relationship with God?" This book describes Chris's journey of asking those questions and the path they took at Experience Life Church to answer them. Chris is one of the trailblazers for the North American Church who is learning from movement leaders who have seen hundreds of thousands, even millions, of new disciples made, using biblical principles and applying those in the North American context. I am privileged to have seen the strategy and principles work firsthand. Since 2006, I have dedicated my life to launch Disciple Making Movements, starting in San Jose, California, and have seen them go viral to more than fifteen countries, producing more than 120,000 new disciples of Jesus in the last four years alone. I highly recommend this book. If you are a follower of Jesus with a desire to experience things similar to what we read in the New Testament, this book is for you.

HERMIE SMIT
Disciple Making Movements Coach
Cityteam Ministries

Reading Chris's book was like having my own personal coach. I was continually discovering new ways to put DMM principles into practice. As a couple, we sensed God filling our sails with new wind. God wasn't finished with us yet! We thank God for allowing us to discover these biblical principles. Our prayer lives and ministry will never be the same. Our faith in God has grown as well as our obedience to the fulfillment of the Great Commission by seeking to make disciples who make disciples who make disciples.

GRANT FERRER
Missionary and DMM Implementer with
Christian Missions in Many Lands
Guadalajara, Spain

I've had the opportunity to watch Chris's leadership over the past ten years of his ministry. More significantly, as his brother-in-law, I've had the privilege of watching his life. And he practices what he preaches. There are few I've met who desire as much as Chris does to see the gospel of God preached to those who have never heard it. His apostolic heart is clear in all that he does. I pray this book will serve to nurture that same heart in all who read it.

BEAU HUGHES
Senior Pastor
The Village Church Denton

Many are becoming more aware of the increasing ineffectiveness of the church in the West in the areas of evangelism and discipleship. What has worked for several hundred years is no longer effective. Few, however, have had the courage not only to address the status quo but to take risks to bring about real change. Chris and others at Experience Life have done this. In this book you will get an honest inside look at Chris's thought processes and the personal costs and risks he and others have taken to see a Kingdom Movement in their city. This is a must read for those of us who desire to partner with God to start Disciple Making Movements in their city but need the encouragement and insight from someone who has gone before us.

DAVID HINMAN
DMM Catalyst and Trainer for Multiply Vineyard

Chris has been a huge inspiration to me as a follower of Jesus and a pastor. His heart for prayer and his risk to rekindle what it means to be a true New Testament church has stretched me to my core. This book will take you back to our roots as followers of Jesus, and then it will take you forward to what is possible in the power of Jesus' name!

BRAD WHITE
Senior Pastor
LifePoint Church

In his new book Pastor Chris describes his journey of rejecting Christian complacency and looks to the Bible and the emerging churches in Africa and Asia for ways to reach the world for Christ. Having started a fellowship in his living room in 2007 with only 12 people, he saw 13,337 people make commitments to Christ in only ten short years, but he believes that God has called us to do so much more.

I have worked in China for the last twenty years and have been an eyewitness to the massive revival there of millions coming to Christ every year. In his book Pastor Chris accurately outlines the pure simplicity and power necessary to evangelize the most unreached people groups and see the fulfillment of Matthew 24:14. This book is a tenacious and bold approach to ministry that requires faith with guts.

EUGENE BACH
Back to Jerusalem

From
MEGACHURCH
to
MULTIPLICATION

A Church's Journey Toward Movement

CHRIS GALANOS

Forewords by Stan Parks and Roy Moran

Cover Design & Illustration by Jesse Owen (10AM Design)
Interior Design by Kristy Edwards Design

Note: Some names have been changed throughout the book to anonymize people in these stories by their request, for security reasons, or because of the particular story.

978-1-7328696-0-8

wigtakedmm.com

Table of Contents

Acknowledgments xiii

Foreword by Roy Moran xv

Foreword by Stan Parks, PhD xvii

Introduction 1

Chapter 1: What Is WIGTake? 3

Chapter 2: 1,000,000 in 10 Years 9

Chapter 3: The Whiteboard 15

Chapter 4: Millions 23

Chapter 5: What Is DMM? 27

Chapter 6: The Ten-Year Anniversary 37

Chapter 7: Leverage 43

Chapter 8: Where's Chris? 51

Chapter 9: DMM Coaching 57

Chapter 10: DMM Training 61

Chapter 11: Raise the Sails 65

Chapter 12: Focus on God's Word 69

Chapter 13: Multiply Extraordinary Prayer 77

Chapter 14: Go Out Among the Lost 85

Chapter 15: See Groups Start 91

Chapter 16: Cast Vision 95

Chapter 17: Train Believers 101

Chapter 18: Ongoing Coaching 105

Chapter 19: Akachi 111
Chapter 20: Andrew and Kristin 115
Chapter 21: From Microsoft to Ministry 129
Chapter 22: Seminary Elective 135
Chapter 23: From Simple to Complex 139
Chapter 24: Identity Crisis 145
Chapter 25: A Reduction in Giving 151
Chapter 26: A Reduction in Attendance 155
Chapter 27: Doubts and Discouragement 163
Chapter 28: PIPSY 169
Chapter 29: Poor 177
Chapter 30: International 191
Chapter 31: Prisoner 207
Chapter 32: Sick 215
Chapter 33: Tentmaking 221
Chapter 34: Weekend Planning 227
Chapter 35: Ty 235
Chapter 36: Shayne 241
Chapter 37: DMM Push Week 249
Chapter 38: How to Get Started (Church Staff) 255
Chapter 39: How to Get Started (Church Attendees) . 263
Chapter 40: Can This *Really* Happen in America? . . . 267
Epilogue: Our Progress 277
Questions for Discussion 281
Appendix 1: Seven-Question DBS Process 297
Appendix 2: Creation to Christ Passages 299
Resources 301
Notes 303

Acknowledgments

To my wife, Emilie: Thank you so much for supporting me and standing by my side through each vision and dream God has given to my team and me. You're my best friend, and none of this would be possible without you. I love you!

To my parents, Gary and Peggy: You guys taught me to chase God-sized visions and to pray and never give up. Your love and passion for Jesus set me on fire for him as a teenager, and I wouldn't be here without you.

To my Executive Pastor, John: Thank you for being willing to chase this crazy, God-sized vision with me. Your friendship means the world to me. Thanks for always leading by example!

To the eLife staff: Thank you for your courage. For the last ten years you've led with faith and bravery as we've seen thousands of lives transformed by Jesus. Let's keep being courageous in the next ten years!

To all of the people at eLife: Thank you for being willing to do whatever it takes to raise the sails that we might see a movement of one million disciples made in the next ten years!

To my eLife church planting coach, Sam: Thank you for believing in me and taking a chance on me when I called you in Fort Worth out of the blue. God has used you in my life in huge ways.

To my DMM coach, Stan: Thanks for believing in eLife and taking the time to train and coach us. We wouldn't be here without you. Thank you for exposing me to the principles that have always been in my Bible but I hadn't seen clearly until recently.

To my DMM mentor and fellow DMM pioneer, Roy: You are the ultimate connector. Thank you for connecting eLife to so many people and resources that helped us on this journey. Thank you for leading the way in implementing DMM in the American church.

To my friend and DMM practitioner, Victor: Your coming to eLife's ten-year anniversary celebration meant the world to me. I pray that what has happened in your country through your leadership will happen in America. I want the whole world to hear your story.

To one of the fathers of DMM, David Watson: Thank you for coming out to see our staff when we first became interested in DMM. Thanks for taking my phone calls over the years and for inviting me to your house when I was nearby. I'm so grateful for your friendship. I, along with other DMM pioneers in the American church, stand on your shoulders in pursuing movement.

To my editor, Alee: You were such a strong encouragement through this entire project. I'm so glad the Lord crossed our paths. I have no doubt that this project is so much better because of you.

Foreword by Roy Moran

While on vacation I took a phone call from a young man who wanted thirty minutes of my time to ask about the journey I had been on with Shoal Creek, a local church I had the privilege of starting with a few people in my living room twenty years before. We talked for more than an hour. My fault, not his!

Five minutes into the conversation, I knew three things about Chris: he is a carnivorous learner; he is hopelessly addicted to building Jesus' kingdom; and for a megachurch pastor, he is refreshingly humble. I am privileged to call Chris and his tribe friends, and I continue to enjoy every moment of interaction with them.

Chris's story is a story in the making. He has given us the privilege of an insider's view of what happens when a megachurch does the Kingdom math and realizes that the law of entropy sentences them to raising more and more money for less and less impact.

The story is true and sometimes not so pretty. But having sat with many of the world's movement leaders (a technical term that refers to those who've planted the good news of Jesus in such a way that it grew to multiple generations over multiple streams in a short period of time), I know firsthand that the stories are never pretty. There are dips, twists, and turns that require learning from mistakes; an unwillingness to throw in the towel; and a willingness to pivot quickly based on new learning.

Changing the direction of any organization is difficult, but a local church has its own set of issues that makes it unique and most difficult to overhaul the culture. Chris and his team have a ruthless faith that causes them to allow no structure to stand in the way of following Jesus' command to plant reproducing communities of obedience to Christ and his commands.

You are holding in your hand the first of many editions of what God is up to at eLife (Experience Life Church in Lubbock, Texas). Chris, John, and their team are addicted to both learning and execution. I am in love with the spirit of eLife! They are not half-hearted by any measure when it comes to following Jesus, and the trail they are blazing will be well-worn by many in the future.

I can't wait to see what God does with Chris's story!

Roy Moran
Author of *Spent Matches*
Senior Leader at Shoal Creek

Foreword by Stan Parks, PhD

I have often wondered what it would have been like to be alive during the days of the early church. In recent years I have actually seen "book of Acts" type movements in some of the "hardest" places in the world. I have seen and can report that "the blind see, the lame walk, those with leprosy are cured, the deaf hear, the dead are raised to life, and the Good News is being preached to the poor" (Matthew 11:5).

The fastest-growing church in the world today is the Iranian church, and the second-fastest growing is Afghanistan. The largest Church Planting Movement in the world is in India, which until recently was known as one of the hardest places to reach. I have the privilege of knowing leaders from these movements, and they describe what God is doing in terms that would be very similar to what Paul and the early believers said when "people throughout the province of Asia—both Jews and Greeks—heard the word of the Lord" (Acts 19:10) and "the message about the Lord spread widely and had a powerful effect" (verse 20).

Numbers represent lives and are important, but they do not paint the total picture. What is also exciting about these movements is how each and every member is given a vision and is equipped to make disciples and plant churches. Many endure great persecution and see God working great miracles. The following are a few examples:

- A woman who became a follower of Christ forgiving the man who murdered her family, and they now work together as part of a ministry serving those unreached with the gospel.
- A man who had been a Muslim religious leader for twenty-eight years publicly proclaiming his faith in Christ at great risk, and as a result most of his village has come to faith.
- A nineteen-year-old man in India who was freed from demon possession, and now he and his sister have planted eight churches.
- God raising back to life the wife of a village chief who had died, and many in that village and region have now heard and trusted the word of God as a result.

Now pause for a minute . . . Did you just read these sentences and think, *That can't really be happening . . .?*

Why not? Jesus said that we will do greater things than he has done!

Or perhaps you read those sentences and thought, *Well, that is great—I am sure that can happen in Africa and Asia, but it cannot happen here.*

Then this book is for you!

Why shouldn't the book of Acts happen anywhere and everywhere today? Why not where you live? Why not see God break loose today in Lubbock, Texas, and West Texas?

The believers described in this book are at the beginning of this journey toward Disciple Making Movements. They are putting aside human tradition and letting God show them how to make disciples. Despite many bumps in the road, God is doing some amazing things in their lives and the lives of those around them.

These believers have been working hard to let God teach them and empower them. They believe disciples should multiply disciples and churches should multiply churches and leaders should multiply leaders. They think they have the same Father to teach them (John 6:44) and Holy Spirit to guide them and empower them (John 16:13; Acts 1:8) as the New Testament disciples did. So why not see God do the same types of mighty movements he did in Acts?

As you read this book, ask yourself, "Would I like to see God work in my life the way he worked in the New Testament and is working today around the world?" If so, we would love to help you make this shift in your life and your church.

Stan Parks, PhD

Movement Catalyst

Serving with 2414 (2414now.net) via Beyond (Beyond.org)

Introduction

This book is the culmination of a twenty-year journey. It takes you from when I was first set on fire for Jesus at the age of sixteen all the way to the present, although not necessarily in chronological order.

While I cover some of what happened during the first ten years of Experience Life, the church my wife and I started in our living room, the focus of this book is more on the second ten years of Experience Life, which are just beginning.

If you were to walk into our church during the first ten years and then walk in now, you'd probably feel as if you'd entered two totally different churches. And you'd be right.

Why the change? That's what I'm hoping to share.

The focus of *From Megachurch to Multiplication* is Disciple Making Movements (DMM). You'll learn more about what those are in the following pages.

This book is not a thorough explanation of DMM, though. For that, I'd encourage you to read several well-written DMM books that I'll recommend throughout. Instead, this is a story about one particular church's journey into the world of DMM.

I believe the unique contribution of *From Megachurch to Multiplication* to the ecosystem of DMM books is the story of our transition from being one of the fastest-growing churches in the United States to a church now focused primarily on "raising the sails" for movement, regardless of what that has meant for attendance.

I pray that our story inspires leaders to consider a similar journey in their own churches. I also pray that our story is an encouragement to Christians everywhere who long to be used by God in extraordinary ways.

This book is just the beginning of our story, and if it encourages you, I hope you'll continue to follow our journey at wigtakedmm.com.

Last, my team and I are available to help and serve you in any way we can. Please feel free to contact us anytime at info@wigtakedmm.com!

I hope you'll consider joining us in "raising the sails"!

Chris Galanos

Lubbock, TX

November 2018

Chapter 1

What Is WIGTake?

L et me formally introduce myself. My name is Chris
Galanos, and I'm the Lead Pastor of Experience Life in
Lubbock, Texas.[1]

Experience Life, or eLife as we like to call it, is a church
that my wife and I started in our living room in April of 2007.
I had just graduated from Southwestern Baptist Theological
Seminary in Fort Worth, Texas, and we felt God leading us to
come back to my hometown to start a new church.

At our first meeting, we had twelve people in our living
room. We prayed that the Lord would allow us to help 10,000
people commit their lives to Christ in the next 10 years. We
all thought the prayer was a crazy one; but we knew that "with
God everything is possible" (Matthew 19:26), so we started
praying with as much faith as we could muster.

Fast-forward to our eighth year as a church, and we
surpassed 10,000 commitments to Christ. At our ten-year
anniversary in September of 2017, we celebrated 13,337 people
who indicated they had committed their lives to Christ and
6,756 who had been baptized during those years.[2]

These verses shared at our anniversary celebration
expressed how we all felt about the last ten years:

3

Now all glory to God, who is able, through his mighty power at work within us, to accomplish infinitely more than we might ask or think. Glory to him in the church and in Christ Jesus through all generations forever and ever! Amen. (Ephesians 3:20–21)

God had accomplished infinitely more than we asked or could've imagined. We thought 10,000 in 10 years was impossible, and God exceeded that number in 8 years. Glory to God!

During year 8, after we passed 10,000 commitments, I started asking the Lord, *What do you want our vision to be for the next ten years?*

That's when I stumbled upon WIGTake.

As I was reading David Garrison's book *Church Planting Movements: How God Is Redeeming a Lost World*, these two sentences leaped off the page at me and almost immediately changed my life: "In the years that followed, Langston was joined by Calvin and Margaret Fox. Together they planned what it would take to reach all of the Kui with the gospel."[3]

Whoa! What?!?! Langston and the Foxes were missionaries to the Kui people group. Together, Garrison says, "they *planned what it would take* to reach *all of the Kui with the gospel*" (italics mine). They didn't plan to just start a church and reach a few people. They developed a plan to reach *all* of the Kui with the gospel. They were willing to do whatever it would take! Do you know how many Kui there are? According to the Joshua Project, a website that breaks down each country into the many different people groups that live in that country, there are 1.6 million Kui.[4] They were developing a plan to reach all 1.6 million! All I could think was, *Wow!*

I immediately thought, *They never taught me this in*

seminary. Typically, you're taught to start a church or get hired at an existing one and hopefully grow the church over time using traditional methods. The plan is usually to reach a few hundred people or maybe a few thousand. But I had never heard of anyone developing a plan to reach an entire people group with the gospel. I wondered if it was even possible.

> *They developed a plan to reach all of the Kui with the gospel.*

When I started eLife, I was hoping just to reach my high school friends and a few hundred others. I wasn't thinking about how to reach my whole city, much less my whole people group.

I started asking the Lord, *In the next ten years, do you want us to develop a plan to reach our whole people group with the gospel, as Langston and the Foxes did?*

I kept reading in Garrison's book, and I continued to see this pattern of aiming to reach an entire people group. "In the late 1980s, three missionary families gathered a few Maasai believers and began to develop a plan to reach all of the Maasai people."[5]

These guys too? They weren't planning to build a church and just reach a few Maasai. These missionaries were planning from the beginning to "reach all of the Maasai people." I couldn't help but wonder what kind of faith is required to think that way.

"By May of 1997, David had developed and implemented a comprehensive strategy to reach all quarters of Addis with a Church Planting Movement."[6] David developed a "comprehensive strategy" to reach how many in Addis? *All quarters* of Addis! As I read through the book, I saw this theme repeated again and again.

Then, later in the book, Garrison introduces the WIGTake question that these missionaries were clearly asking. He credits David Watson with initially forming the question for his work among an unreached people group in India. David Watson asked, "What's it going to take to reach 90 million [in this unreached people group] in this [twenty-year] generation?"[7]

What's it going to take to reach everyone in the people group?

The WIGTake question is: "What's it going to take to reach everyone in the people group?"

Not, "What can I do?" or, "What can you do?" Not, "What have others done before us?" Not, "What's possible?" No. "What's it going to take?" That's the question we must ask! We have to be willing to do whatever it's going to take! After all, that's our commission.

> Jesus came and told his disciples, "I have been given all authority in heaven and on earth. Therefore, go and make disciples of all the nations, baptizing them in the name of the Father and the Son and the Holy Spirit. Teach these new disciples to obey all the commands I have given you. And be sure of this: I am with you always, even to the end of the age." (Matthew 28:18–20)

Jesus told these guys to make disciples of how many nations? What did he want them to aim for? *All the nations!* Search on the internet for how many people were in "all the nations" at the time of this writing. What did you learn? About two hundred million, right?[8]

Now put yourself in the disciples' shoes.

Jesus has just been raised from the dead, he's about to ascend into heaven, and he's about to tell you what he wants you to spend the rest of your life doing. He essentially says, "I want you to go and make disciples of two hundred million people. And don't freak out at the task; I'll be with you as you go."

If I'm a disciple, I am definitely freaking out. I am thinking, *Jesus, there's no way we can reach two hundred million people. That's crazy! How are we supposed to do that?*

His reassurance was simple yet profound: "I'll be with you."

Even the disciples were told to develop a plan to reach the world—not just to start a church, buy a building, hire a preacher, and hope it grows over time.

Needless to say, the WIGTake concept, combined with Matthew 28, rocked my world. I spent months wrestling with it and talking with the Lord about it. Eventually these conversations with God led to a complete change in the direction and vision for our church for the next ten years. And when the vision changes, so does the strategy.

When the vision changes, so does the strategy.

Chapter 2

1,000,000 in 10 Years

What's it going to take to reach everyone in our people group?

This central WIGTake question led our Leadership Team into a season of prayer and fasting about the direction of our church for the next ten years. It's a powerful question. It's also a scary question. I had never asked it before. *We* had never asked it before.

First, we had to figure out who the second part of the question refers to. How many people are actually in our people group? None of us knew.

Once again, we turned to the Joshua Project for help.[1] After all, your people group isn't typically just the total population of your country. Most countries have many different people groups who speak different languages, come from different places, and have different cultural backgrounds. According to the 1982 Lausanne Committee Chicago meeting, "For evangelization purposes, a people group is the largest group within which the Gospel can spread as a church planting movement without encountering barriers of understanding or acceptance."[2] Based on that definition you could see how a country could have many, even hundreds, of different people groups.

According to the Joshua Project, the United States has 488 people groups among the more than 325 million people who live there. The two largest people groups listed are the ones most Americans belong to, and the total population of those two people groups is approximately 225 million.[3] This means 100 million people in our country are not technically in our people group as we've defined it.

We decided to use 225 million as the size of our people group. According to the very helpful research done by John S. Dickerson in *The Great Evangelical Recession*, approximately 22 to 28 million Americans can be classified today as Evangelical Christians (we'll use the average of 25 million as our number), leaving 200 million people we would be aiming to reach. (Note: Our numbers have been rounded as closely as possible for vision casting purposes.)[4]

That's right. There are 200 million people in my people group, in my country, who need Jesus and whom I'm able to share with in an understandable way. Wow! In learning this for the first time in our lives, our hearts broke not just for our friends or our neighborhood or our city or our region, but for our entire people group. We couldn't help but pray the same as missionaries all over the world, *Lord, would you allow us to be a part of reaching all of them? Not just some. Not just the ones who live near us. But all of them?*

Second Peter 3:9 says, "The Lord isn't really being slow about his promise, as some people think. No, he is being patient for your sake. He does not want anyone to be destroyed, but wants everyone to repent." We knew the Lord doesn't want anyone to be destroyed but wants everyone to repent. We felt that we were praying according to his "revealed will" in asking that everyone would be reached!

Reaching everyone is what John Langston and the Foxes would aim to do if they were sent here as missionaries.[5] That's what the three missionary families to the Maasai would aim to do.[6] That's what David Watson, who took the gospel to the unreached in India, would aim to do.[7] That may not be what traditional American pastors, such as myself, aim to do, but reaching everyone is the aim of missionaries all over the world. They are desperate to see entire people groups come to know the Lord. Shouldn't we be as well? When God sent these missionaries to a people group, they developed a plan to reach everyone. We should do the same.

David Watson, when he went to the unreached people group in India, went a step further and planned not just to reach *all* ninety million in the people group, but he planned to reach them in "this 20-year generation!"[8]

Missionaries are desperate to see entire people groups come to know the Lord. Shouldn't we be as well?

So I began to ask: What would it take to reach the 200 million in our people group in twenty years? If you assume multiplication and work backward from 200 million in twenty years, you'd need to reach 1 million people in the next ten years to be on track to reach the 200 million in the next twenty years.

I remember the day we sat down as a Leadership Team and talked about this. I was excited to bring the idea to the team, but I had no idea how they'd react. And yet, when I announced the idea, and we went around the room, everyone agreed that we had to do whatever it took to reach 1,000,000 people in the next 10 years. Together, we decided to develop a plan, agreeing wholeheartedly that this is what God wants us to do with the next ten!

The meeting was monumental. It came out of months of prayer and processing (for some of us *years* of prayer and processing). You could feel the excitement in the room.

If God accomplished the "10,000 in 10 years" vision in eight years, which seemed totally impossible to us when we first started praying about it, what might God do if we asked him for 1,000,000 in the next 10 years?

We joked about how going from twelve in a living room to 10,000 in 10 years was asking God to give us one thousand times what we had in that living room at our first meeting, while asking God for one million in ten years was only a hundred times what we had reached at the end of the first ten. For a minute we wondered whether our prayer was too small. One person even suggested we pray for ten million. Needless to say, we stuck with 1,000,000 at the end of the day.

1,000,000 people in the next 10 years. That became our prayer, our vision, our passion, and our drive. It became our Romans 15 ambition: "My ambition has always been to preach the good news where the name of Christ has never been heard, rather than where a church has already been started by someone else" (verse 20).

Just as the disciples in Matthew 28 had their number of 200 million, we now had our number of 200 million as well. And we knew we needed to aim for 1,000,000 in the next ten years to be on track. We also knew we couldn't do it alone. We needed other churches, denominations, networks, and organizations to join us. Together, we could aim for everyone!

Our WIGTake became: *What's it going to take to reach 1,000,000 in the next 10 years so that we're on track to reach 200 million in 20 years?*

Figuring out the second part of the WIGTake question,

namely the size of "everyone in our people group," was the easy part. Determining the first part of the question was going to prove to be a lot more difficult. And I mean a lot more difficult.

What's it going to take to reach 1,000,000 in the next 10 years?

"What's it going to take . . ." to reach all of those people? We knew that figuring out what it was going to take would require us to count the cost. We knew we would be required to give up some things we had cherished for years. We knew it would require us to think about "church" differently and even do "church" differently than we ever had before. We knew that some people wouldn't want to make the journey with us, even people we loved and had been with us for years. We knew that giving could drop dramatically, and we'd have to make difficult cuts in the budget. We counted this cost before we moved forward and believed that our sacrifice would be worth it. We all believed that following Jesus was worth any cost.

Chapter 3

The Whiteboard

W e had our number. We now knew the size of our people group, and we knew what we needed to pray toward for the next ten years.

Now for a deep dive into the first part of the question—*What's it going to take?*

On a Thursday afternoon, after our weekly staff prayer meeting, our Leadership Team was gathered in our conference room, and I wrote "1,000,000" at the top of the whiteboard and asked the team, "Any ideas how?"

It was natural for us to start with the idea of continuing to do what we had done the past ten years because it had worked so well for us. We had a multi-site church of ten campuses with thousands attending each weekend. Our methodology was attractional. Designed with lost people in mind. Aimed toward using the weekend to reach as many people as possible. We had a great band, and we played a mix of worship music and music you'd hear on the radio. The sermons consisted of topics relating to practical issues that many in our culture would be facing. You probably know of a church that's similar to ours. You've probably *been* to a church that's similar to ours. And I'm guessing you have an opinion about it too!

In the last ten years, eLife connected with many people. We had 54,168 first-time guests who completed a connection card and many more who never filled out a card, I'm sure.

As the church grew, we started more campuses, hired more staff, and spent more money. You know—all the things that typically happen when churches grow. American churches, that is.

As we thought about the number of campuses, buildings, staff, and money that would be required for us to reach a million people in the next ten years, we were baffled. We decided to try to come up with a calculation.

The average cost per baptism in the typical American church is . . . you may want to sit down for this . . . $1.5 million.[1] Yes, it costs, on average, an estimated $1.5 million per baptism in the American church. In other words, if you take all of the income American churches bring in each year and divide it by the number of baptisms, you get this number. Feel free to gasp in disbelief.

> *The average cost per baptism in the American church is $1.5 million.*

Roy Moran, one of my DMM coaches and author of *Spent Matches*, refers to this same statistic and argues that if our strategies cost this much money, perhaps we should reconsider how we are attempting to reach people. Even if we could afford that amount, Moran argues, it probably wouldn't matter because our strategies haven't proven to be effective at reaching our growing population.[2]

eLife's Executive Pastor, John Bradshaw, who is also a CPA, keeps careful track of all of the money that flows in and out of our church. We asked him to determine how much each baptism at eLife has cost in the last ten years. His figure: $5,000. That's still expensive, but at least it wasn't $1.5 million.

We thought, *Okay. Let's work out a rough estimate of what it would cost us to reach one million people, using our current model, by multiplying the cost per baptism by the number of people we want to reach.*

Oh gosh.

$5,000 X 1,000,000 PEOPLE = $5,000,000,000

Our cost per baptism number is pretty low comparatively, but we'd need at least $5 billion in the next ten years to reach one million. That's not even accounting for the difficulties involved in finding the staff and facilities, managing all of it, and so forth.

It took us about thirty seconds to toss that idea.

We all thought that if God really wants us to pursue the million, there's no way we can continue the strategy of the first ten years. It's not going to work; it's way too expensive. Way too difficult. Way too . . . everything.

On top of the financial and personnel issues, as Roy Moran indicates, is the American church model even working the way it's supposed to? As a national church, are we accomplishing our mission?

> We all thought that if God really wants us to pursue the million, there's no way we can continue the strategy of the first ten years.

Before you respond, I'd encourage you to consider the research in the fascinating book *The Great Evangelical Recession* by John S. Dickerson.[3] The subtitle of the book gives an idea of its direction: *6 Factors That Will Crash*

17

the American Church . . . and How to Prepare. The factors are troubling, to say the least.

Lest you think this is just another sensationalist author, John S. Dickerson is an award-winning investigative journalist turned Senior Pastor who has written essays and opinion columns for *USA Today,* CNN, the *New York Times,* and the *Washington Post.* Dallas Theological Seminary (DTS) had him speak in their chapel service on this topic. The president of Phoenix Seminary wrote an endorsement for his book. This guy is legit.

In the first chapter, Dickerson highlights several of the factors "that will crash the American church" and then spends the rest of the book diving into each of them:

> The evangelical church in the United States is not nearly as large as we've been told. This might not seem like a big deal, but it's a huge deal . . .
>
> Overestimating the size and "value" of the evangelical church is—much like housing prices—one of the silent triggers, one of the unexamined fault lines under the Great Evangelical Recession.
>
> In a moment, I'll explain just how much we have overestimated our size. But first, a word on why it matters. In the coming chapters, we're going to see irrefutable data. We'll see that . . .
>
> • the fuel of American evangelicalism—dollars— is disappearing and will dwindle over the next three decades.
> • we're losing millions of our own people—about

2.6 million per decade, just from one generation
studied.

- the evangelical church is not winning new
  believers fast enough to keep pace with rapid
  population growth in the United States.
- while these forces eat at the church internally, the
  external climate is turning against evangelicals.
  The fastest growing subcultures in the United
  States express a militant antagonism against
  Christians who take the Bible seriously.
- what's left of a smaller, shrinking, strapped church
  is also splintering and splitting itself over politics
  and postmodern views of God and the Bible.[4]

Dickerson's book argues persuasively that the American
church is in trouble. Many of us realize that we're bleeding out
as a church, but I don't think I was aware of the extent until I
read this book.

Dickerson points out how remarkable it is that the enormous amount of money given to evangelical churches hasn't
kept them from shrinking. Even though billions of dollars
are given to churches and ministries across our nation, the
evangelical church is still unable to keep up with population
growth in our own country. We have more wealth than at any
time in history, yet we can't even hold our ground at home.
When will we accept the fact that "many of our best efforts
are not only failing, but actually backfiring"?[5]

Based on his research, Dickerson concludes:

> If we want to rebuild and restore a culture of dis-
> cipleship, we have no choice but to release the way

American church was done in the 20th century. The late-20th-century church model, in so many applications, requires so much energy and attention that little to nothing is left for anything else, including discipleship. The 20th century church model which revolves around buildings, weekend gatherings, sermons and such is not primarily focused on discipleship. Discipleship gets crowded out because doing all of those things takes so much time. We do all those things hoping we get discipleship, but it doesn't seem to be working.[6]

I think anyone who has pastored an American church longer than a year knows there is a lot of truth in Dickerson's conclusion.

I had our Leadership Team read this book, and we started jokingly calling it "The Great Evangelical Depression"! However, even though the book leaves you a little depressed about the state of the American church, it ends up formulating a hopeful solution to the problem.

I thought the concepts in the book were so important that we did a four-part message series on it at eLife called "Meltdown: The Decline of the American Church."[7] People in our church were shocked to hear Dickerson's research and were greatly bothered by the negative trends.

Dickerson is not the only one sounding the alarm. He's one of many.

Thom Rainer is the president and CEO of LifeWay Christian Resources and an evangelical researcher. Sam Rainer is the president of Rainer Research. Separately, they concluded, "Most churches are dwindling. Most denominations are not growing. The population in the United States is exploding . . . the church is losing ground. We are in a steep state of decline."[8]

In *The Fall of the Evangelical Nation: The Surprising Crisis Inside the Church*, Christine Wicker writes, "Evangelical Christianity in America is dying. The great evangelical movements of today are not a vanguard. They are a remnant, unraveling at every edge. Look at it any way you like: Conversions. Baptisms. Membership. Retention. Participation. Giving. Attendance. Religious literacy. Effect on culture. All are down and dropping. It's no secret."[9]

Wicker is correct. It's definitely not a secret. Most pastors I know admit Wicker's statement is true and are bothered by it. Many of us would admit that the American church model is on life support, but what do we do about it? Are there any other options?

The Leadership Team and I went back to the whiteboard.

Looking at the "1,000,000" number written at the top of the blank board, we continued to come back to the same question: If our existing American church strategy can't get us to the million, is there a strategy that can?

As our team sat there, we were all thinking the same thing. We knew of a strategy. We had heard the stories. We had been reading books about them for months. We had talked about them for years. We had even visited some of these places. But the stories weren't from here. They weren't from America. They were from India, Africa, and China.

Millions were coming to Christ. We couldn't help but ask, *Could God do the same thing here?*

Chapter 4

Millions

I remember receiving the annual report a few years ago from one of our church's mission partners in India. We had partnered with these people for years in their work among the unreached.

Our partner's results were astounding—so astounding, in fact, that help was needed to measure the impact. Outside research teams had to be hired to try to calculate the number reached.

Typically, when we receive a yearly report from this partner, the researchers will give three different numbers to estimate the size of the movement. They will give a low, mid, and high estimate, since no one can be sure of the exact count due to its enormous size and constant, favorable change.

I pulled up the report excitedly and saw this:

- Low estimate: 8 million baptized believers
- Mid estimate: 10 million baptized believers
- High estimate: 12 million baptized believers

By the opinion of an outside research team, not our

partner alone, this movement had grown to between eight to twelve million people meeting in hundreds of thousands of house churches over a twenty- to thirty-year period.

Remember the cost per baptism in the United States? $1,500,000.[1] Guess what the cost per baptism is in this movement. 66 cents.

The cost is virtually nothing to reach all of these people.

I'd love to give you more information about this particular movement, but for security purposes, this must suffice for now. However, I can tell you that missionaries had gone to this place for centuries with minimal impact until this movement of God broke out a few decades ago. It's growing so quickly there's no telling how many will eventually be reached.

We have another mission partner working among the unreached in China.

In the 1950s under Mao Zedong's dictatorship, China kicked out all the missionaries and closed all the church buildings. Thousands of pastors were imprisoned and eventually killed. Mao's wife, Jiang Qing, told foreign visitors, "Christianity . . . has been confined to the history section of the museum. It is dead and buried."[2] In the 1970s, a Christian group visiting from the United States reported, "There is not a single Christian left in China."[3]

Even in the midst of much persecution, China has perhaps seen one of the greatest movements of God in history. Since the 1970s, some researchers estimate that more than one hundred million people have become disciples of Jesus and are meeting in hundreds of thousands, perhaps even millions, of house churches.

Our partner was instrumental in this season of growth and was imprisoned, beaten, and almost killed for preaching the gospel. What has happened in his country in the last fifty years is remarkable.

We have some friends in an African country who have seen some amazing things happen in the past ten years. The country where they live is more like America than the other countries I've mentioned. Their country is majority Christian. Nominal Christian, that is. Much like America. Traditional Western-style churches were everywhere, but they weren't reaching very many people. That is, until recently. In the last ten years, they estimate that more than one million people in this region have become disciples of Jesus.

Did you notice a word that was used to describe each of these stories? *Millions.* Not thousands. *Millions.*

Our Leadership Team knew about each of these stories. After all, several of them come from mission partners of our church. They would visit us regularly and tell stories about all that God was doing. And we had been reading their books.

> *In the last ten years, they estimate that more than one million people in this region have become disciples of Jesus.*

Over the prior three months, I had asked the Leadership Team to read three books. These books were three of many through which God had spoken to me in previous years. I wanted to see if God would say the same thing to our Leadership Team that he said to me.

These books were:

- *The Great Evangelical Recession*[4]
- *Spent Matches*[5]
- *Church Planting Movements*[6]

As we looked at the "1,000,000" number on our whiteboard

again with these books and stories in mind, we all knew there was a strategy that could take us to the million. It was a foreign strategy. Foreign to America, that is.

The strategy is not foreign to church history. It's the strategy of the early church. You see, this strategy is detailed in the Gospels and in the book of Acts.

We knew this strategy could take us to the million because that same strategy had taken many of our friends to many more than a million disciples. And it's the only strategy we know of that has the potential to reach millions. It has done it over and over again.

The problem was, we only knew of one other church in all of America who was even attempting to implement it.

Could it work? Could God do it here? Could we see in our country what our friends have seen in theirs? Could we see millions?

> Could we see in our country what our friends have seen in theirs? Could we see millions?

In that moment, God gave all of our Leadership Team the faith to say, *Yes!* We knew God could do it here too! We just needed to ask him to do it and plan for it to happen, just like many missionaries have done.

You may be wondering, *What's this strategy you're talking about?*

Enter DMM.

Chapter 5

What Is DMM?

D MM stands for Disciple Making Movement. This acronym is closely related to CPM, which stands for Church Planting Movement.

While I will attempt to give a brief explanation of these concepts in this chapter, you'd be best served by reading the following books for a more detailed explanation:

- *Miraculous Movements*[1]
- *The Kingdom Unleashed*[2]
- *Spent Matches*[3]
- *Church Planting Movements*[4]
- *Contagious Disciple Making*[5]

In chapter 4, I mentioned that we have several friends in other parts of the world who have witnessed the making of millions of disciples in a short period of time. Missiologists (those who study missions) call these incredible works of God "movements" or, specifically, "Church Planting Movements."

David Garrison, author of the book *Church Planting Movements*, argues that Church Planting Movements are the most effective means for seeing millions all around the world come to Christ, and God appears to be using them to do just that.[6]

A Disciple Making Movement is one of the strategies that can lead to a Church Planting Movement. DMM is the strategy employed by several of the friends I referred to in the previous chapter. Let me share a few definitions of Disciple Making Movements from reputable sources so that you get an idea of what I'm talking about.

According to Stan Parks, a DMM Trainer and Vice President of Global Strategies at Beyond, "DMM is obedience-based discipleship that sees disciples reproducing disciples, leaders reproducing leaders, churches reproducing churches, and movements reproducing movements."

Roy Moran, author of *Spent Matches,* says,

> DMM is a strategy that has six key character-istics: God ordained, Spirit dependent, Bible centered, obedience focused, discovery based, and disciple driven. In brief, DMM turns average followers of Christ into event planners, rather than salesmen for Jesus, so that they can invite their friends, neighbors, and workmates into small groups designed to hear from God through reading the Bible, obeying what He says, and sharing it with their social networks.[7]

According to Jerry Trousdale in *Miraculous Movements,* "In a nutshell, Disciple Making Movements spread the gospel by making disciples who learn to obey the Word of God and quickly make other disciples, who then repeat the process.

This results in many new churches being planted, frequently in regions that were previously very hostile to Christianity."[8]

To better understand the concept, it's helpful to know how DMM measures success. How people measure success says a lot about why they do what they do.

For many American churches, including ours at times, *success* is having as many people as possible fill the seats at worship services on Sundays to hear teaching from God's Word. That explains why churches hire a staff to facilitate those services. That explains why those staff members spend their whole week planning for the services and the programming surrounding the services. That explains why churches need to raise a lot of money from the congregants to fund the salaries for those staff members. That also explains why buildings are so important. A place is needed to have these worship services. And the money, often millions of dollars, is needed to be able to build and maintain these facilities.

What most people don't know, especially in America, is that what I have just described is quite an unusual way of doing church in parts of the world where the church is expanding rapidly through Church Planting Movements. It's what most of us grew up with, so we assume everyone does it. But doing church that way is so expensive and difficult to reproduce that it could never keep up with a rapidly growing movement. In fact, some movement practitioners argue that these things can actually kill Church Planting Movements. As a result, people in growing movements are often warned that on the rare occasions when churches in other movements have started trying to fund these things, they often stop reproducing.

Those who implement a DMM strategy measure success differently. In most places where DMM is implemented, churches don't even have traditional "weekend services" like in an American church, so they're unconcerned with many of the things I mentioned previously.

To those executing a DMM strategy, success can be summed up in two words: *generational discipleship*. They measure whether disciples are making disciples who make more disciples who make more disciples. As disciples are being made, churches are intentionally being planted with these new disciples. They don't plant churches hoping to get disciples (which is what I did). They make disciples, and from those disciple-making efforts, churches are planted.

To those executing a DMM strategy, success can be summed up in two words: generational discipleship.

In fact, an active "movement" is often defined as multiple streams of fourth-generation churches among previously lost people, adding up to at least one hundred new churches in two to four years.[9] Sunday attendance, money in the offering plates, and participation in programs are not counted. Instead, those who implement a DMM strategy are counting generations of disciples and churches.

To be clear, four generations of churches planted among lost people would look like this: A church planting team makes disciples and sees Church #1 planted among previously lost people. Church #1 makes disciples and sees Church #2 planted among previously lost people. Church #2 makes disciples and sees Church #3 planted among previously lost people. Church #3 makes disciples and sees Church #4 planted among previously lost people. That's four generations of church planting.

To clarify, if Church #1 plants four churches, that's not fourth-generation growth. All four of those churches are second-generation churches. It's best to think of generational growth like generations in families. Four generations would be like great-grandparent to grandparent to parent to child. I'm the fourth generation from my great-grandfather.

You might be thinking, *Wow, if generational growth really happens, I can see how these movements would grow so quickly.* Right! Because the focus isn't on addition—it's not about adding people to a weekend service. It's about multiplying disciples. Numbers grow much quicker through multiplication than addition.

In fact, there are more than 650 active movements in the world today, and the average size is more than 75,000 believers. Think about that. The average movement is larger than the largest American church. Wow!

So, you ask, how does this strategy work? I encourage you to pull out your Bible and read Matthew 10 and Luke 10. The strategy comes from these chapters—the same strategy Jesus gave his disciples when he sent them out.

> *The average movement is larger than the largest American church.*

Begin with prayer. Ask the Lord to show you the place he has prepared for you to go (Matthew 10:5–6; Luke 10:1). He may lead some people to leave their town and go somewhere else; but for many, he'd have us go to a place in our very own town. For ideas of where the Lord might send you, see chapter 28. We don't just randomly pick a place to make disciples. God has already been working to prepare a place for us to go—we just need to open our hearts to hear from him so we can join him where he's working. And guess who's praying and preparing to go? Ordinary believers. Not just pastors. Not just people on a church staff. Movements unleash ordinary people to make disciples and plant churches. That's part of what makes movements so different from a typical American church.

Once the Lord has shown you the place he wants you to go, begin to pray specifically for that place (Matthew 9:37–38; Luke 10:2). Often, disciple makers will spend weeks, or even months, "prayer walking" the place, asking God to open the hearts of people there.

Movements unleash ordinary people to make disciples and plant churches.

Next, begin to look for the *person of peace* whom God has prepared to receive the gospel (Matthew 10:11; Luke 10:5–6). The person of peace will become the one who will spread the gospel to his or her own community in a culturally appropriate way, using language that will be understood. Notice, at its core, DMM is not a "come and see" strategy. It is absolutely a "go and tell" strategy. Instead of trying to get lost people to attend church services, which most lost people don't want to do anyway, you're taking the gospel directly to them.

Then begin to meet needs in this area, and share about Jesus while doing so. Jesus said that after you enter this new place, "Heal the sick, and tell them, 'The Kingdom of God is near you now'" (Luke 10:9; also see Matthew 10:7–8). You could meet a need by praying for the sick, as Jesus described, or meet a practical need that could open someone's heart to the gospel. Doing these things often reveals the person or household of peace. Stan Parks says, "Around the world, the number one way DMMers find those interested in God is by serving them (healing prayer, kind deed, community service) while consistently, simultaneously, and culturally appropriately pointing to God."

Once you find a person or household of peace who welcomes you and receives your message, begin a discipleship process with that person or household (Matthew 10:7–8; Luke 10:8–9). This discipleship process is not what you'd typically think of in the American church. You don't bring in a teacher to start a series of Bible studies. Rather, you do what Jesus talked about in John 6:44–45. You invite the person or household of peace to listen to the Father and learn from him because "everyone" can be taught by God through his Word (verse 45). Jesus said that if people listen to and learn from the Father through his Word, then the Father will draw them to Jesus (verse 44). A group where the members discover for themselves, with the Holy Spirit as the teacher, what God says through his Word, is often called a Discovery Group (DG). The members of the group discover what God wants them to know and obey by asking a series of questions about the passage they're reading:

1. What does this teach us about God?
2. What does this teach us about people?
3. If this is from God, what should we do/obey in response?
4. Who should we share this with?

The Holy Spirit speaks to the members through the Word as they ask these questions. The emphasis is on immediate obedience (hence, obedience-based discipleship used in the DMM definitions mentioned previously) and sharing with others. Typically, a Discovery Group will start with passages from the Old Testament that will take the members from creation to Christ. Often, as a group begins to read, the Father draws the members to Jesus (as he said would happen), and the whole group commits to Jesus as Lord and is baptized together. Then the members begin to learn how to function together as a new church.

This new church obeys the Great Commission in Matthew 28:19–20 and begins to go out making more disciples and repeating the process all over again (Matthew 10; Luke 10), thus creating the next generation of the church.

Someone might ask, how do people in these movements define church? It's simple: Acts 2:36–47. That's what Stan Parks said when I asked him that same question.

Remember, these churches aren't typically large groups of people who meet in expensive buildings. They often meet in homes or other places where groups of people naturally gather, just as the church did in the New Testament. The average size of these churches worldwide is fourteen believers, according to Stan.[10] Occasionally these churches will cluster in groups of fifty to one hundred for encouragement and training, if the context permits.

> *The average size of these churches worldwide is fourteen believers.*

What are DMM churches like? One leader in a movement overseas said that he'd put these churches up against any church in the West, in terms of commitment to God's Word, church health, courage in the face of persecution, or any other category.[11]

Further, Beyond, a missions-sending organization, recently posted a series of videos corresponding to the CPM steps, which I've found helpful in giving an introduction to this strategy.[12] To summarize, CPM steps are as follows:

Step 1: Prayer
Step 2: Prayer Walking

Step 3: First Contact

Step 4: Miracles and Healings

Step 5: Discipleship

Step 6: Reproduction[13]

Since our Leadership Team knew that God was using DMM all over the world to reach millions of people, we believed it was the strategy we needed to execute in the next ten years. Although it was not a strategy typically used by churches in America, we knew God had led us to this strategy. He revealed it to us in his Word and through the testimony of other believers around the world. As a result, we came to believe it was the only strategy that could take us to the million. Our team was united, and we had our marching orders from Jesus for the next ten years.

The next step was announcing it to the entire church at our ten-year anniversary celebration!

Chapter 6

The Ten-Year Anniversary

We were so excited to let our church know about the vision for the next ten years. We decided that our upcoming ten-year anniversary service on September 10, 2017, would be the time to make the announcement. It would be the first time in almost ten years that all ten campuses would be together in one service.

Since we knew the announcement would be such a big one for our church, we decided in the months leading up to the anniversary to do a few sermon series to help set the stage for the announcement.

The first series in January 2017 was called "Meltdown: The Decline of the American Church."[1] As I described in chapter 3, this series was influenced by the book *The Great Evangelical Recession.*[2] In order to justify a complete change in strategy and direction, we needed to begin by demonstrating the need for a change. This sermon series dealt at length with how the American church is in trouble, and how unless something changes, it could be heading for a great crash.

A few months after that series, we decided to do a series on what we believed was the solution to the problem, DMM.

We called this series "Miraculous Movements," named for the book by the same name, and spent a whole series telling stories about the great Disciple Making Movement happening right now in Africa.[3]

We believed those two series would generate excitement and enthusiasm in preparation for the big reveal at the ten-year anniversary.

When the day of the anniversary service arrived, we were all thrilled to meet together in one place. We rented out the Lubbock Municipal Coliseum, which could host up to six thousand people. We had everyone from all ten of our campuses gather for one big service to celebrate what God had done in the first ten years and to cast the vision for where we felt God was leading us in the next ten.

I stepped up to speak at the service, and I told the church about our friends around the world who are seeing millions come to Christ. In fact, some of them had traveled across the world to be with us that day. It was such an honor to have them there!

Then I told the church that our Leadership Team sensed God leading us to pray for 1,000,000 disciples in the next 10 years. I asked the church if they believed God could do it, and the question was met with loud applause. If God blew away our "10,000 in 10 years" vision, we had no reason to doubt that he could do the seemingly impossible again in the next ten years.

I emphasized that DMM invites every ordinary believer, not just pastors, to be a disciple maker and church planter. Although ordinary people being disciple makers isn't particularly controversial, ordinary people *acting* as church planters may be a bit controversial in our country. This is not the case in countries where DMM is succeeding in making millions of disciples. I explained further how believers often refer to themselves as church planters in these movements when people ask what they do. They'll say, "I'm a taxi driver to provide for my family, but I'm actually a church planter." Or, "I'm a schoolteacher to make a living, but I'm actually a church planter." In these countries, ordinary believers think of themselves as church planters because they see it as *their* job to make disciples and to see churches planted. They don't just view it as the job of their pastor.

> In these countries, ordinary believers think of themselves as church planters because they see it as their job to make disciples and to see churches planted.

To explain how DMM can reproduce so quickly to reach millions of people, I shared with the church an analogy using elephants and rabbits. This analogy was introduced to me through the DMM Catalyst Training that I went through a few years ago.

It goes like this: Imagine you have been asked to feed a village that is running out of food. You are given an estimate that in three years the village will face starvation. Would it be better to give the people in the village two adult elephants or two infant rabbits to help them avoid starvation?

What would you say?

Unless you grew up around rabbits, you'd probably go with the elephants because they're a lot bigger, and theoretically you'd think the food supply would be greater. But you'd be mistaken.[4] Here's why.

Elephants	Rabbits
Only fertile 4 times per year	Practically continuously fertile
Only 1 baby per pregnancy	Average of 7 babies per pregnancy
Mother carries baby for 22 months	Mother carries babies for 1 month
Age when you can have a baby: 18 years	Age when you can have a baby: 4 months
3 years: 2 elephants become 3	3 years: 2 rabbits become 50,643
3 years: 26,000 lbs. of food	3 years: 661,000 lbs. of food
5 years: 2 elephants become 4	5 years: 2 rabbits become 69,000,000
5 years: 38,000 lbs. of food	5 years: 925,000,000 lbs. of food

Rabbits reproduce so quickly and elephants so slowly that elephants could never produce as much food as the rabbits, not that you'd want to eat either, though!

Now think about this illustration in terms of church strategies. Elephant churches are traditional American churches. They're big. They usually have a building. They require lots of money. They require a staff. They are hard to reproduce due to stifling, traditional growth strategies. Rabbit churches are small churches, often meeting in homes. They are led by ordinary, unpaid believers. These rabbit churches are found in the rapidly growing movements all around the world.

After sharing this illustration, my DMM trainer, Stan, said, "Elephant churches are strong and helpful, but they reproduce so slowly that we need more rabbit churches to truly reach the world."

DMM author Jerry Trousdale said, "God bless elephant churches; they serve wonderful functions. But from every strategic perspective, megachurches and even average-sized churches will never fulfill the Great Commission without a goal and plan to launch thousands of rabbit churches. Only a rabbit church has the ability to reproduce rapidly, thrive in a dangerous environment, and naturally facilitate obedience-based discipleship within every member."[5]

I then told the church that eLife is clearly an elephant church; and, of course, we all love the elephant. But if we want to reach 1,000,000 people in the next 10 years, not only do we need elephant churches, we also need rabbit churches if we expect to get the job done.

If an average rabbit church has twenty members, we'd need to see 50,000 churches started in the next ten years to reach the million. Then, working backward, I shared that if we need 50,000 churches in year 10, we need 25,000 churches in year 9; 12,500 churches in year 8; and so on. Continuing to work backward, that meant we needed to plant 50 churches in our first year. With that math, the million stopped feeling so unattainable.

I then announced that we had just finished training our first 54 church planters to leave our church and go plant these rabbit churches.

We need rabbit churches if we expect to get the job done.

We asked the 54 rabbit church planters to come to the stage; and our church gathered around them, prayed for them, and commissioned them to go out, make disciples, and start churches!

It was a powerful moment that symbolized what we were praying for in the next ten years. The excitement and sense of anticipation in the room was at an all-time high. We couldn't wait to see what happened next! But that left us asking, *What do we do with the elephant?*[6]

Chapter 7

Leverage

T he weekend after our ten-year anniversary, I shared with our church the Leadership Team's desire to leverage every ministry to help accomplish this new vision. We want to leverage weekends, groups, youth ministry, children's ministry, and everything else to help us see 1,000,000 people become disciples in the next 10 years. Then I said, "That means things are going to change!"

What we did in the first ten years was great, but it wasn't going to take us to the million. Not only did we want to send out rabbit church planters, a.k.a. DMM Church Planters, we wanted to reevaluate everything we were doing in light of the new vision.

As you might imagine, not everyone likes change. When you announce that change is coming, some people think, *This is awesome! I love trying new things and taking new ground!* Whereas others probably think, *Oh gosh! I don't want to change! I love what we're doing now!*

I asked each staff member to pray and ask the Lord this question: *Lord, how do you want me to leverage the ministry I lead to help accomplish the vision you've given us for the next ten years?*

People started coming up with great ideas. We didn't know whether the ideas would be fruitful, but we said we were willing to try anything. We knew we wouldn't figure out how to best leverage each individual ministry area unless we took risks and tried new things.

We started asking the same question about our weekend services. How can we leverage the weekends to help us accomplish the vision of the next ten years?

My guess is that weekends are probably people's least favorite thing to change. Many people who grew up in American churches enjoy the way the weekend services are run, and they don't like to have the format changed. Worship. Announcements. Sermon. Dismissal. If you mess with that, you're messing with something people grew up with. But, of course, we weren't going to keep doing something just because "that's the way we've always done it." We wanted to leverage the weekends in whatever way the Lord would lead.

As I shared in chapter 5, while Western-style weekend services are common in traditional *churches* around the world, they are not very common in many of these *movements* around the world. As a result, I wasn't sure exactly how to properly and effectively leverage an American weekend service because there weren't many movements around the world using them. We needed the Lord to show us.

I remember getting on my knees one Saturday afternoon and saying to the Lord, *What do you want us to do on the weekends? We know that weekends aren't essential in DMM because not many of these other movements use them, but could our weekends be helpful? We have many people coming already, and it seems that we could leverage these weekends to help with the vision. What do you want us to do? You're our Senior Pastor, and we want to hear from you!*

I really sensed the Lord put some things on my heart as I prayed, so I quickly grabbed a pen and began to write them down. The first thing he brought to my mind was what I've heard over and over again during the last twenty years. Henry Blackaby, author of *Experiencing God*, has said it, and my dad reminds me of it all the time[1]: prayer and testimony are the fuel of revival.

> *Prayer and testimony are the fuel of revival.*

If you study revival history, you'll see that God has used prayer and testimony over and over again to set people ablaze. An example would be the Asbury Revival of 1970 at Asbury College in Wilmore, Kentucky.[2] There were many professing Christians at that school, but they weren't on fire for God. They were lukewarm and living in sin. There was a general consensus among the students that they needed revival.

Thirty-six students joined together in an experiment. They covenanted together to spend thirty minutes with Jesus each morning for thirty days. They would read and obey the Bible. They would pray. They would share their faith. They would meet once a week to keep each other accountable and to pray corporately.

They scheduled an all-night prayer meeting for the night before the experiment would be over. When college students get together to pray all night, rather than party all night, something is about to go down!

While the students had planned to pray all night, at 2:30 a.m. someone said they believed God was going to visit them in their chapel service the next morning and they all should go home and get some sleep. The next morning, on Tuesday,

February 3, they went expectantly to the 10 a.m. chapel service.

The dean of the college stood; but instead of speaking, he shared his testimony, then opened up a microphone and invited others to do the same. Five minutes before the end of the chapel meeting, a philosophy professor told the dean, "God is here. If you give an invitation, they'll come."

The dean invited students forward to confess their sins and to publicly recommit their lives to following Jesus. A flood of students responded and came confessing theft, cheating, resentment, jealously, lust, worldly attitudes, prejudice, pride, and hatred, among other sins. Broken relationships were reconciled as students went to one another to ask for forgiveness. Many described this atmosphere by saying that it was as though Jesus had walked through the door of the auditorium. There was nowhere else anyone wanted to be.

The chapel service didn't end that day at 11 a.m., when it was supposed to. It didn't end at 2 p.m. that day or 4 p.m. It didn't even end late that night or the next morning. It lasted 158 hours straight and didn't end until Tuesday of the next week.

Word spread quickly, and people traveled from all over the country to witness this gathering. People would arrive, sense the presence of God, confess their sins, and recommit their lives to him. This revival impacted cities all across the nation.

What was the fuel? Prayer and testimony!

In the first ten years at eLife, we mainly had songs, announcements, and sermons, like most American churches. But for the next ten, I sensed the Lord saying that he wanted us to spend even more time praying together and sharing testimonies of how he was working in our lives. In other words, I sensed God leading us to "open the mic."

The second thing God brought to my mind is something I've heard about around the world but have never really seen modeled in the American church. It's this: movements don't happen unless people are reading, obeying, and sharing the Word of God.

I knew our church had the reading part down. We would read and teach from Scripture every weekend. But Jesus didn't

> *Movements don't happen unless people are reading, obeying, and sharing the Word of God.*

say to just teach people. Notice what he told his disciples in Matthew 28:20: "Teach these new disciples to obey." Don't just teach them stuff. Teach them to obey the commands he's given us. Teach them to literally follow Jesus! That involves *obeying* and *sharing*, not just learning.

For most of us, when we think of teaching or sermons, we think of information transfer. A speaker gets up on stage and teaches us new information. We get bored when we're not learning anything new. Pastors feel a lot of pressure to constantly come up with new things to teach. People demand new content. That's not what Jesus said to do. Jesus said to teach the new disciples to *obey*. In movements overseas, it's called *obedience-based discipleship*. The focus isn't on information accumulation. The focus is on life transformation through *obeying* Jesus and *sharing* about him with others.

In our context, the word *teaching* doesn't have the connotation of obedience at all. A better word, perhaps, if we want to communicate that we desire to teach to obey, is the word *train*. Training implies obedience or application.

Think about job training. As you take on a new job, you're

observing as somebody does a task you will eventually be doing yourself. Usually it's not in lecture format. Lecture format doesn't tend to produce application the way being with a mentor does, watching him or her perform a task, and then letting that person watch you and correct you along the way. That's teaching to obey.

I felt that the Lord wanted us to focus more on teaching to obey, or training, in the next ten years, not just teaching for information transfer.

I've asked friends in these movements around the world, "What's different between our churches and your churches?" One of the things I hear over and over again is, "You guys focus on knowledge. We focus on obedience." These friends call what we had been doing *knowledge-based* discipleship and what they do *obedience-based* discipleship. Their words stung a little, but I knew it was true.

In case it stings you a little too much, and you feel the urge to resist that characterization, I'd encourage you to think about this: In the American church, how do we decide when to move on to the next sermon or the next Bible study lesson? We move on once we've heard it, read it, or learned it, regardless of whether anyone has obeyed it. In fact, we would be insulted if the pastor preached the same sermon he preached last weekend because we didn't obey it the first time. Or if our Bible study leader said the group would be repeating the lesson from last week because we didn't obey it. In traditional American churches, obeying is not the goal. We move on once we've *learned*, not once we've *obeyed*; hence the term *knowledge-based discipleship*.

But in many DMM churches overseas, guess how they decide when to move on? When they've obeyed! In fact, they will often repeat the same lesson until everyone has obeyed it.

One of our friends, a leader in a movement that has reached millions, said the movement's motto is, "Learn one thing. Do one thing." Then they move on. That's always stuck with me. They don't learn the second thing until they've done the first thing. They don't move on until they've obeyed. That's a prime example of obedience-based discipleship. In fact, you could argue that spiritual growth in the New Testament is measured not by whether you've learned but by whether you've obeyed (Matthew 7:24–27; Philippians 4:9; James 1:22–25).

> *"Learn one thing. Do one thing."*

PRAYER. TESTIMONY. TRAINING.

As I was praying that day about how to leverage our weekends, those were three of the things I sensed the Lord saying to me. I discussed it with our Executive Team and we began to leverage our weekends that way. Since then, the Campus Pastors design their weekend services around prayer, testimony, and training.

The strategy for the next ten years is definitely different from our strategy for the first ten, but it's going to take something different to reach a million people with the message of Jesus.

It's worth noting here that some pastors who have been on a journey similar to ours have not tried to leverage the weekend services at their churches. Instead, some have led their churches through the process of closing down their traditional church to plant many more churches in a different way.[3] Others have humbly resigned from their position as

Senior Pastor and moved on to making disciples outside the traditional American church. A recent example of this second approach is Francis Chan. He left the megachurch he pastored to start a network of house churches that he believed better resembled what he saw in the New Testament. He just released an excellent book called *Letters to the Church* that explains his reasoning for leaving his church and the way he is currently seeking to make disciples.[4]

The Lord leads people in different ways during different seasons. He can lead a church in one way now and a different way in the future. For now, at our church, we sensed the Lord leading us to leverage the weekends for movement so that many of the people who journeyed with us through our first ten years could join our new journey in the next ten years.

Chapter 8

Where's Chris?

"Where's Chris?" That's actually a popular question at our church these days! You see, in the first eight years or so of eLife, I preached almost every weekend. That's what I was supposed to do, right? I had started a church. I was the Senior Pastor. Senior Pastors preach pretty much every weekend. Right?!?! That's definitely what I thought for a while.

As eLife grew, we began to add services. At one point, I was preaching five services every weekend—two on Saturday and three on Sunday. To be honest, it was exhausting.

I called a friend of mine at a large church who used to preach that many times each weekend and asked for advice. He said, "You've got to stop, bro. I used to preach five services, but it about killed me. I've dropped back to four now—two on Saturday and two on Sunday. You need to slow down."

Needless to say, I needed to hear that. We made some immediate changes and pulled the preaching back down to four services and eventually three.

As the years went by, I started to wonder if having just one primary teacher was healthy for me or the church. I couldn't really find anything in the Bible that said one guy should preach all the time. In fact, I found quite the opposite. Acts 15:35 says, "Paul and Barnabas stayed in Antioch. They and many others taught and preached the word of the Lord there."

As it turns out, Paul wasn't the only one preaching the Word in Antioch. Barnabas preached alongside him. But it wasn't just Paul and Barnabas who preached in Antioch. Look at what the second part of that verse says. "They [Paul and Barnabas] and many others taught and preached." It wasn't just Paul and Barnabas and a *few* others who preached. Paul, Barnabas and *many* others preached. Guess what *many* means in the original language? It means "many"! As in *a lot of people*! There were a lot of people preaching and teaching there. Not just one guy.

The Acts passage doesn't say people complained. It doesn't say people demanded that Paul be the only speaker (which would make sense if they did because it's *Paul*, for crying out loud). It also doesn't say that everyone left when Paul stopped speaking.

Why is that? I think it's because people were more excited about the message than the messenger. The message had the power! The Word of God had power! People wanted to hear God's Word, regardless of the messenger!

People were more excited about the message than the messenger.

If I can be honest—and this is true even in my own life—it seems that in the American church we are often more excited about the messenger than the message. We often choose a church based on the talent of the messenger. We change churches when the messenger isn't as good as he used to be or we don't like the new messenger's style as much as that of the previous messenger.

Almost any research based on surveys of church attendees will show that the most common reason a person chose their church is that they liked the messenger. I'm not saying that's all bad. I'm not saying we need to pick a church with a terrible preacher. I'm just pointing out that in the American church we've placed our focus on the messenger more than the message. Once again, that's an American phenomenon and not the case everywhere else in the world.

In my humble opinion, this has contributed to a "celebrity preacher" culture in America. And, unfortunately, we're seeing celebrity preachers fall left and right, leaving many people disillusioned. A very famous preacher I've looked up to for years fell into sin and had to step down. It just keeps happening. The power, fame, and influence that can come with these positions can be dangerous. Is this what the Lord wanted for preachers?

So we made a change at our church. I'm not preaching as much as I once did. I don't want to be a celebrity preacher.

We need all of the people of God to be "preachers" of the Word of God! After all, the key to reaching a million people with the gospel in ten years is hundreds and thousands of "preachers" preaching, not just a few "celebrity" preachers. "After this prayer, the meeting place shook, and they were *all* filled with the Holy Spirit. Then they preached the word of God with boldness" (Acts 4:31, italics mine).

> We need all of the people of God to be "preachers" of the Word of God!

You see, the power comes from the Word of God—the message! What has the potential to change people's lives? The Word of God!

The best thing the messenger or preacher can do is to

preach the Word and then get out of the way. Let the Word do the work, "for the word of God is alive and powerful . . . sharper than the sharpest two-edged sword" (Hebrews 4:12–13).

The way you know you're more excited about the *messenger* than the message is when you're upset if your favorite teacher isn't teaching. Perhaps you choose not to attend that day. Or perhaps you choose to switch churches because he's not preaching as much as he used to.

The way you know you're more excited about the *message* than the messenger is when you don't care who's teaching as long as the message is the same. You love and are excited about the message, namely, God's Word! Just like the believers in Acts 15.

I was convicted that in the first ten years I was pretty much the only messenger. In fact, I preached so much in the first ten that I started having vocal issues. I had to travel to Dallas for treatment and take a break for a season. Yet, in Acts 15, Paul, Barnabas and *many* others taught and preached the Word of God. To me, sharing the preaching and teaching duties seemed healthier for me and for our church in the long run.

Once we started solidifying plans for the next ten years, I, and others, wondered whether my vocal issues were perhaps another way the Lord was leading me to slow down and share the responsibility with others. After all, that's what had been modeled for me in Scripture. Maybe I just needed a little push to obey?

Once I started having others help with the teaching, I had more time to pray, lead, read, and cast vision for the future. The decision to start using a teaching team for sustainability and health reasons came a few years before we even began thinking about DMM. I'm not sure if DMM would've even come into the picture if I, and others, hadn't freed up the time to be able to think about it, read about it, and talk to others about it.

I can't imagine what dreams and visions God would give Senior Pastors if they shared the teaching responsibilities and spent more time in prayer, seeking God for his vision for their churches.

For those of you who have never been an "every week preacher," I can say from experience that sermon preparation can consume most of your week. It's hard to do much else. And when you're not just the preacher, but also one of the primary leaders of the church, you need plenty of time to *lead* as well!

Pastors, if people are asking where you are, that might be a good sign that you're sharing the teaching responsibilities, spending more time in prayer, and strategizing with others about how to lead your church to prepare for a movement of God.

Don't fall in love with the messenger! Messengers will let you down. Messengers come and go. You must fall in love with the message. Better yet, fall in love with the Author of the message.

"All Scripture is God-breathed and is useful for teaching, rebuking, correcting and training in righteousness, so that the servant of God may be thoroughly equipped for every good work" (2 Timothy 3:16–17 NIV).

> *Don't fall in love with the messenger! Fall in love with the Author of the message.*

55

Chapter 9

DMM Coaching

I am a big fan of coaching. I think everyone needs a coach. Coaches make you better at whatever you do.

Even professional athletes who have trained their entire lives have coaches. No one has to convince an athlete that he or she needs one. Everyone recognizes that you can be better in business, in sports, and in virtually every aspect of life if you have someone helping you continually hone your craft. The same is true for churches.

When we were preparing to start eLife eleven years ago, I knew I needed a church planting coach. I had no idea how to plant a church. I had never done that before. I remember getting a flyer one day in chapel at my seminary about a guy named Sam Douglass who was coaching church planters.[1] I held on to that flyer and decided to give him a call. And when I called, he said he'd love to help.

Sam and I started meeting on a regular basis at a donut shop in Fort Worth, and he walked me through the process. He taught me how to put together a proposal for the new church. He taught me how to approach people and raise money. He taught me some of the strategies I could use to start the church. He walked with me all the way through our launch, and he has continued to do so through the first ten years.

Originally I had planned to start a church in either Frisco, Texas, or Round Rock, Texas, but it was Sam who challenged me to consider going back home to Lubbock to plant a church.

Without Sam I wouldn't be where I am today. I definitely wouldn't be in Lubbock. God has used him in my life in a tremendous way over the past ten years. Not only has he been a pastor to me, but he has been someone who was always available for a phone call if I ever had any questions or difficulties. He's exactly what you'd hope for in a coach.

As eLife began venturing into the world of DMM, I knew I needed another coach. I had never been a part of a Disciple Making Movement before. All I knew about DMM was what I had read. Thanks to my relationship with Sam, I knew a coach could help me get started, avoid pitfalls, and guide me through the process.

One of our mission partners I wrote about in chapter 4 has a staff member who lives here in Lubbock. That staff member happened to attend our church. When he heard I was becoming interested in some of what was happening overseas, he said, "Chris, Stan is a DMM coach who has learned from and partnered with our movement. He is going to be in town soon; would you like to meet with him?"

I said, "Absolutely!"

I thought, *If this coach is connected to that movement, and they've reached more than ten million people, he could be exactly the guy I'm looking for.*

I met Stan a few weeks later, and we connected immediately. After spending a day with our team, I knew Stan was someone our team needed to stay in touch with. We met a few more times, and I felt he would be the best coach for us in our church's next season. The only problem was that he was already coaching movement leaders all over the world and was highly sought after. I didn't know if he'd be willing to coach us, since we were just getting started and really hadn't borne much fruit. Plus, he lived in Dubai and wasn't in the United States much. The majority of our coaching would have to happen via video conferencing.

I still thought I would ask him and see what he said.

When Stan said yes, our team was thrilled! We considered it such a great privilege to be coached by someone of his caliber. We thought his availability would be a long shot, but I'm so glad we asked. We knew he would be able to help us get started, avoid common mistakes along the way, and answer our questions as we ran into difficult situations.

We asked Stan what he wanted us to do first as we moved toward DMM. He said he wanted to take us through a twelve-week DMM Catalyst Training. This training was based on principles God had used around the world, and Stan would just pass on biblical lessons he had learned from David Watson and many other movement catalysts.

Stan told us he had taken a husband and wife team, who were missionaries in another country, through the very same training. After embracing the training and beginning to implement it, this couple saw more than five thousand churches planted in their first four years. And this was in a very difficult part of the world.[2]

Stan told us several other amazing stories of what had happened

> *This couple saw more than five thousand churches planted in their first four years.*

59

when people implemented this type of DMM training: hundreds of thousands or even millions of difficult-to-reach people coming to Christ.

We couldn't wait to get started. Little did we know that this training would radically change our lives and the lives of many others.

Chapter 10

DMM Training

When Stan said he was going to take us through a twelve-week DMM Catalyst Training, I said, "Great! Can you send it to me?"

He said, "Nope."

I asked, "Why not?"

Stan then made it clear that this training was not information to be transferred but biblical principles to be obeyed. The focus wouldn't be on learning, like most Bible studies. Instead, the focus would be on obeying. This wasn't just another piece of typical American curriculum. He told me he'd send the sheet of paper after he took us through each lesson, but he wouldn't send all twelve lessons at once.

As it turned out, most of the trainings could fit on one sheet of paper and sometimes wouldn't even take up the whole sheet. The reason was that most of the training was just lists of Bible passages that Stan would have us reread with fresh eyes. And you can't even imagine what rereading these texts with fresh eyes will do for you. You come to realize, once again, that the Word of God truly is *alive* and *powerful* and that its principles are *timeless*!

> *The Word of God truly is alive and powerful, and its principles are timeless.*

Stan didn't outwardly explain this practice of waiting until the end of the lesson to give us the training sheet, but after going through the training and taking others through it, I understood.

Because I come from a knowledge-based discipleship culture, as most of us do, my tendency would be to read the twelve lessons and think, *Okay, I've got this; let's move on.* But, again, this wasn't information Stan wanted to transfer; these were biblical principles he wanted to coach us to obey! That means you don't even need to look at lesson 2 until you've obeyed the passage from lesson 1. Stan was going to make sure from the very beginning we weren't distracted by "learning"—he wanted us laser-focused on obeying.

At the end of each lesson, as promised, Stan would send us the sheet he used for that lesson; and it was remarkably simple. Typically, it included just a few Bible passages, some questions to ask about the passages, and perhaps a few comments.

The DMM training definitely does not follow the same formula of a typical American Bible study. In fact, it's so simple, readers might question the simplicity, thinking, *I already have this Bible study. It's called the Bible!*

As we started the training, I was encouraged to toss all of my extrabiblical baggage and everything I *thought* I knew about how to make disciples and how to do church out the window. I was definitely willing to do that. After all, even though our church was certainly regarded as a "successful" one by American standards, we knew that our American strategy wouldn't allow us to impact millions. I decided to assume I knew absolutely nothing so that I could take a fresh look at the Scriptures without dragging along all of my Western assumptions.

As our training continued, I began to notice something strange. Stan didn't talk much. He told us that the Holy Spirit would speak to us as we took a fresh look at these Bible passages; he didn't want to interfere with what the Holy Spirit wanted us to hear and obey.

Most of the time when Stan spoke, he asked us questions about the text we were reading, trying to get *us* to think and talk. Sure, he told us some stories that fired us up. He prayed for us regularly. He guided our discussions so that we didn't get offtrack. But, besides that, Stan just listened as we discovered from God's Word things that had been there all along but that we had never noticed before.

Stan wanted us to see the DMM principles in Scripture so we'd be dependent on God, not on him. And we definitely saw Scripture in a whole new light! During those twelve weeks, our world was totally rocked!

Once Stan led us through a lesson, we immediately passed it on to another group of people, which Stan said is very important in internalizing the training and beginning to apply it immediately.

Remember the story in chapter 9 about the couple who started 5,000 churches in their first four years after implementing the DMM training? Well, at the time of this book's publication, the couple is now seven years in, and that 5,000 has multiplied to between 25,000–30,000 churches planted with hundreds of thousands of new believers.

This couple is not unlike other missionary couples who for years had done traditional compassion ministry overseas but weren't seeing the traction they'd hoped for. They were helping many people but not making disciples, which felt like the missing piece of the puzzle. That led them to go through the very same DMM training as our team, and it totally changed their lives and the way they think about ministry and making disciples. This couple's focus is now 100 percent on disciple making; and, as you can see, the result is hundreds of thousands of disciples in a relatively short amount of time. It all started with this husband and wife team going through DMM training and inviting a DMM coach to mentor them through the process.[1] Their story encouraged us to begin praying that God might use us in a similar way.

Chapter 11

Raise the Sails

The next seven chapters will break down the seven elements involved in "raising the sails" for a movement.

Stan introduced the notion of the seven elements of "raising the sails" in our DMM training. He explained that these elements are found consistently in the lives of ordinary believers who are successfully making disciples in these movements all over the world.

That definitely got our attention. It would be critical to make sure the seven elements were lived out by our staff, our church, and our DMM teams.

Before we talk further about the elements, I wanted to dig into the concept of "raising the sails." Stan shared it with us in lesson 2, calling it the *Sailboat Analogy*. It goes like this: A sailboat doesn't get movement without the wind. The wind is the most important element in sailing, and if no wind is present, you aren't going anywhere. The same is true with a movement of God. A movement cannot happen without the wind of the Holy Spirit. He is absolutely the most important factor in seeing a movement of God break out. Without him, there is no movement.

But something else is also true. If there is plenty of wind, but your sails aren't up, you aren't going sailing either. You may get a little movement, but not the kind you want. You won't have any idea where you're going. If you want to go sailing, you not only need the wind, you need to raise your sails. The same is true with movements of God. A movement of God doesn't happen without the wind of the Holy Spirit, but a movement also doesn't happen if the wind of the Holy Spirit comes and you don't have your "DMM sails" up!

A movement cannot happen without the wind of the Holy Spirit.

Therefore, if you intend to go sailing, you need one thing you can't control and one thing you can: the wind and raised sails. You can't control the wind of the Holy Spirit, but you can control whether your DMM sails are raised when the wind of the Spirit comes!

As we take a look at the seven elements in "raising the sails" for movement, we see that we are talking about the part we can control. We want to get our sails up! That's not to say that by getting our sails up the wind of the Spirit will blow into them immediately. We don't control the wind. God does. But we want to get our DMM sails up so we're ready whenever the wind of the Spirit decides to blow!

We want to get our DMM sails up so we're ready whenever the wind of the Spirit decides to blow!

Once Stan explained the Sailboat Analogy and introduced the seven elements to us in lesson 2 of the DMM training, he repeated the elements at the beginning of every lesson from that point forward. In fact, he had *us* repeat them after the first few times. That's how important they are. These elements were ingrained in our minds by the time the training was over. The seven elements formed the framework by which we understood and implemented DMM.

One thing Stan said again and again throughout the training is that we must raise the sails for movement and encourage others to do the same. You don't want just a few people "raising the sails;" you want as many as possible!

The Sailboat Analogy made so much sense when I first heard it, and our team has returned to it over and over again. We don't bring movements. God does! We just need to have our sails up for when he comes!

Now let's dive deeper into each of the seven elements.

Chapter 12

Focus on God's Word

T he first element in "raising the sails" for movement is "Focus on God's Word." Most of us hear that and think, *I already do that.* But the way you think of this may not be the same way those who practice DMM think of it.

When we hear "focus on God's Word," chances are we think about reading the Bible, listening to sermons about the Bible, downloading some podcasts where people talk about the Bible, and so on. But that's only one aspect of focusing on God's Word, and it leaves out two other very important things. Simply defined, focusing on God's Word involves a regular pattern of reading, obeying, and sharing the Word of God.

Many of us have the reading part down. It's the obeying and sharing parts that we often tend to miss, especially in the American church.

> *Focusing on God's Word involves a regular pattern of reading, obeying, and sharing the Word of God.*

Roy Moran, in his book *Spent Matches*, agrees with this, saying:

Jesus asked followers to teach people to obey all of His commands. What have we done in response? We've taught people all of Jesus' commands and assumed that knowing them means they will obey them. Many people—believers and nonbelievers—would give today's church a very low grade when it comes to obedience to Jesus' commands.[1]

If you've been in the church for a long time, chances are you know a lot about the Bible. Maybe you've read it all the way through a couple of times. You've listened to sermons about it on Sunday mornings for most of your life. You've been in several small groups where you've talked about it. All of that is good, but that alone doesn't "raise the sails" for movement. Remember what Jesus said in Matthew 7.

Anyone who listens to my teaching and follows it is wise, like a person who builds a house on solid rock. Though the rain comes in torrents and the floodwaters rise and the winds beat against that house, it won't collapse because it is built on bedrock. But anyone who hears my teaching and doesn't obey it is foolish, like a person who builds a house on sand. When the rains and floods come and the winds beat against that house, it will collapse with a mighty crash. (verses 24–27)

In short, anyone who listens to his teaching and . . . what's the next part? "Follows it is wise"! Other translations say anyone who listens to his words and

- "acts on them" (NASB)
- "puts them into practice" (NIV)
- "does them" (ESV)

What's the emphasis here? The emphasis is not just on listening to the teaching. It is on *obeying* it! *Following* it! *Acting on it! Putting* it into practice! *Doing* it!

I think you get the idea.

Too often we remember Matthew 7:24 as, "We are like people who build our house on solid rock if we listen to Jesus." That's not it—we've got it wrong. A solid foundation doesn't just come from *listening* to Jesus. Many of us are really good at that. It actually comes from taking it a step further and *obeying* Jesus! In other words, it's about obedience-based discipleship, a concept in Scripture that our friends overseas have helped us rediscover. DMM practitioners measure spiritual growth by gauging how much people are *obeying* Jesus, not how much they *know* about Jesus!

The Pharisees *knew* a lot. Jesus didn't give them credit for that. The disciples didn't know as much, but they *followed* Jesus and *obeyed* what he taught (not perfectly). Jesus took a special interest in and gave the Great Commission to the disciples—the ones who acted on what they knew.

Focusing on God's Word is a regular pattern of reading, obeying, and sharing God's Word. Many of these movements around the world use a tool called Discovery Bible Study (DBS) to help those involved focus on and stay committed to reading, obeying, and sharing. Each week they gather as a disciple-making community

The Pharisees knew a lot. Jesus didn't give them credit for that.

71

(a.k.a. church) and ask some version of the following seven questions.

1. What have you been thankful for in the past week?
2. What has challenged or stressed you or anyone around you during the past week?
3. Is there anything this group can do to help with those challenges or stresses, or is there any other need we can meet together?

At this point they'll review the passage of Scripture from the last time they met. A few people will retell the passage in their own words. Then they'll ask the next four questions.

4. What did this passage teach us about God?
5. What did this passage teach us about people?
6. What did you do this past week in response to this passage?
7. Who did you share with this past week?

Doing this helps people to remember the previous passages and also keeps everyone accountable to obey and share each week.

After reviewing the previous passages, if a majority of the group has obeyed, they'll move on to a new passage of Scripture. If the group has not obeyed, they may reread the previous passage and stay focused there until they have helped each other obey. Remember, the goal isn't simply to learn and move on but to obey. It's not helpful to move on until a majority of the group has obeyed.

It's not helpful to move on until a majority of the group has obeyed.

If the group moves on to a new

passage of Scripture, they'll read it (or listen to it) several times aloud together, and then everyone in the group will retell it in his or her own words. Then they'll ask questions 4–7 again about this new passage:

4. What does this passage teach you about God?
5. What does this passage teach you about people?
6. What should you do this week in response to this passage?
7. Who should you share with this week?

One of our friends from Africa told us that question 7 is the most important question if you want to see movement. Without sharing regularly, how will you find "persons of peace" and see new groups started? You won't. Sharing is absolutely essential.

Asking the group questions about the passage of Scripture, rather than teaching them about it, allows each person to "discover" for themselves, with the Holy Spirit as the teacher, what God wants each one to learn. This is exactly what Jesus said would happen in John 6: "As it is written in the Scriptures, 'They will all be taught by God.' Everyone who listens to the Father and learns from him comes to me" (verse 45).

The New Testament teaches a concept often referred to as the "priesthood of all believers." This concept says that the believer can go directly to God and hear directly from him as Jesus said in the above verse. Believers don't need a priest or a mediator because we already have one—Jesus Christ!

As participants in the DBS read the Scriptures, they are "taught by God." They listen to and learn from the Father directly; and, as a result, they are drawn to Jesus!

I have found that people are more committed to truths

they discover for themselves than those they are taught by other people. Luke commended the Bereans for searching the Scriptures themselves to make sure what Paul said was true (Acts 17:11). They wanted to "discover" the teaching for themselves from God's Word, with the Holy Spirit as the teacher.

The Discovery Bible Study (DBS) process invites the Holy Spirit to be the teacher using the Bible as the curriculum. So, guess what? You don't have to be a gifted "teacher" to lead because the teacher is the Holy Spirit. *Anyone* can lead! And that includes you!

All you have to do is read the questions, open the Scriptures, and let the Holy Spirit speak to everyone in the room. In fact, you don't even have to be able to read. In many places around the world where this process is being used, people can't read. Instead, they memorize the questions, listen to recorded scriptures, and the Holy Spirit speaks through the Word of God!

This "discovery process" is bearing fruit all over the world as God speaks to people through his Word as he said he would. And the most powerful part of the discovery process is when the Holy Spirit tells each individual (or the group as a whole) what they should *obey* that week and whom they should *share* with.

It's easy to see how many disciples can be made in a short period of time if people start reading, obeying, and sharing the Word of God. Having said all of that, may I ask you a question? Do you "focus on God's Word" or do you just read it?

Do you "focus on God's Word" or do you just read it?

If I'm being honest, for most of my life, I just read it. Only recently has the Lord opened my eyes to the power of intentionally obeying and sharing it on a regular basis.

Each day as I read God's Word, I no longer just read and move on. I spend time asking the Lord, *What do you want me to obey from what I've read today? And with whom do you want me to share?* Then I write in my journal what the Lord wants me to obey that day and with whom he wants me to share. It's been a life-changing adjustment.

Each of the DMM church planting teams sent out from eLife have goals related to each of the seven elements. The chapters that follow will end with the goals the DMM church planting teams are coached to strive toward—all of the goals that follow can be used by any DMM church planting team working toward movement.

GOALS FOR FOCUSING ON GOD'S WORD

- Meet together each week as a group to "focus on God's Word" by doing the seven-question DBS process.
- Spend five days each week on your own "focusing" on God's Word by reading, obeying, and sharing.[2]

Chapter 13

Multiply Extraordinary Prayer

The second element in "raising the sails" for movement is "Multiply Extraordinary Prayer." If you study some of these movements overseas, one thing that will immediately become apparent is that they pray . . . *a lot!* Let me give you an example from a book called *Miraculous Movements*, which details one of these movements in Africa.

> Here are some characteristics of prayer that we have seen among the hundreds of ministries that we coach and train, and within our own teams.

> - Many Christians pray . . . and fast every week at least two meals in one day.
> - Many new Christians gather regularly for all-night or six-hour prayer vigils.
> - Midday prayers for members of churches and ministry teams are common.
> - Personal disciplines of early-morning prayer are very common. One hour to two or three hours of prayer is not uncommon.

- Family devotions centered on discovering the Bible together and praying together are common.[1]

For most of us that would definitely qualify as extraordinary prayer—adding up to hours of prayer and fasting every week. If we are honest with ourselves, we may notice that we barely pray an hour a month, much less a few hours a day.

In David Garrison's book *Church Planting Movements*, he lists ten elements that are found in every Church Planting Movement. Guess what number one is? Extraordinary Prayer.[2] In fact, Garrison says, "Prayer permeates Church Planting Movements. Whether it's Koreans rising at four in the morning for a two-hour prayer time, or Spanish Gypsies 'going to the mountain,' as they call their all night prayer vigils, Church Planting Movements are steeped in prayer. Consequently, prayer has become the first priority of every Church Planting Movement strategist."[3]

When I began to study movements from around the world, the thing that kept jumping out at me was the desperation for God and how people expressed that through prayer. They wanted to see God touch their nation. They wanted to see all of their family members, friends, coworkers, and neighbors follow Christ. They wanted to see God come and do something miraculous. They believed the key was prayer!

We shouldn't be surprised, right? We see this call to pray throughout the Scriptures. Here are just a few examples from the first few chapters of the book of Acts:

- "They all met together and were constantly united in prayer, along with Mary the mother of Jesus, several other women, and the brothers of Jesus." (Acts 1:14)

- "All the believers devoted themselves to the apostles' teaching, and to fellowship, and to sharing in meals (including the Lord's Supper), and to prayer." (Acts 2:42)
- "Peter and John went to the Temple one afternoon to take part in the three o'clock prayer service." (Acts 3:1)
- "As soon as they were freed, Peter and John returned to the other believers and told them what the leading priests and elders had said. When they heard the report, all the believers lifted their voices together in prayer to God." (Acts 4:23–24)
- "After this prayer, the meeting place shook, and they were all filled with the Holy Spirit. Then they preached the word of God with boldness." (Acts 4:31)

Stan has often said, "When we're asking God for a movement, we're essentially asking him to do again what he did in the book of Acts."

The early church in the book of Acts catalyzed a great movement of God that swept the Roman Empire and led to millions coming to Christ in a relatively short period of time. I'm convinced that if we want to see results like they saw in the book of Acts, we have to do what they did in the book of Acts. And what's one thing they were constantly doing? Praying!

I was so convicted of my own prayerlessness when I saw how my brothers and sisters in Christ all around the world were praying. I

I'm convinced that if we want to see results like they saw in the book of Acts, we have to do what they did in the book of Acts.

felt immediately that the Lord was leading me to challenge our staff to take our "ordinary" prayer lives to the next level. As our Leadership Team was talking to Stan about how "extraordinary" prayer looks and how to implement it, he said, "Your prayer life now is ordinary for you. Add something to it to make it extraordinary for you. Then when that becomes ordinary, add something again to make it extraordinary. Keep repeating the process."

That made sense to us. We already prayed as a staff every Thursday from 1–2 p.m. Most of us also prayed another hour each week with our small groups. I just sensed we needed to be praying *more*.

So I issued a challenge. In a message to our staff, I said, "Let's start praying every weekday for an hour rather than just once a week, much like they started doing in the 1857–1858 Prayer Revival under the leadership of Jeremiah Lanphier." After that, we started praying for one hour through lunch every day.

In addition, I told the staff that our brothers and sisters in Christ overseas pray through the night regularly. Even the *new* believers in some of these movements are trained to pray through the night at least twice each month. Since we're leaders in the church, I told them we needed to start praying at least half the night once every single week.

We settled on Sunday nights. Every Sunday from 8 p.m.– midnight, we pray together as a team! While adding the weekday prayer meetings and the half-night prayer on Sunday night is still much less time spent in prayer than many of our friends in these movements, it is extraordinary for us.

It's not just about "extraordinary" prayer, though; it's about multiplying extraordinary prayer. It's not enough just that *we* pray in an extraordinary way; we want to challenge others to begin to do the same. We want as many individuals as possible asking the Lord how he wants them to increase in prayer.

As we began to encourage others to pray, different groups of people in our church felt God leading them to pray through the night. One person who initially started praying with us on Sunday nights started his own half night of prayer on Friday nights. Then another person started a half night of prayer on Thursday nights. And another person started having monthly *all-night* prayer meetings. Several others started praying for extended periods of time as well.

People started becoming interested in praying for long periods of time together. When that happens, since it's so unusual, and maybe even extraordinary, you know God must be up to something.

We've found that the more we pray, the more we *want* to pray. Several of our staff would say that praying more has set them even more on fire for God. I am reminded of a quote from Jim Cymbala in *Fresh Wind, Fresh Fire*: "The more we pray, the more we sense our need to pray. And the more we sense a need to pray, the more we want to pray . . . When the apostles were unjustly arrested . . . they didn't call for a protest; they didn't reach for some political leverage. Instead, they headed to a prayer meeting"[4] (referring to Acts 4:23–31).

You may be wondering, *Where did all of this half night of prayer and all-night prayer stuff come from anyway?* Luke 6:12 says, "One day soon afterward Jesus went up on a mountain to pray, and he prayed to God all night." I'm sure our friends overseas thought, *If Jesus himself needed to pray all night long, how much more do we need to pray?*

Therefore, there's no doubt that if we want to raise DMM sails for movement, we need to Multiply Extraordinary Prayer—a common element in every active movement in the world today.

Will you allow the Lord to take your ordinary prayer life to an extraordinary level?

I've heard people say that Prayer Movements precede Church Planting Movements. We're definitely trying to catalyze a movement of prayer! Why do Christians in America give so little time and attention to prayer if every great movement of God has been preceded by much prayer?[5] Jerry Trousdale, author of *The Kingdom Unleashed*, wrote,

> Prayer is the lifeblood of movements. The church in the Global North [referring to North America and Europe] does not rely on prayer, and if behavior is any indication, it does not believe in it, either. If we are going to see movements in the Global North, we will need to see a new, ongoing commitment to serious, intense, persistent prayer for God to open heaven, to raise up disciple makers and church planters, to guide us to His people of peace, and to empower our work. Without that, there will be no movements and the church will continue its slow, inexorable decline into irrelevance in Global North culture.[6]

Prayer Movements precede Church Planting Movements.

GOALS FOR MULTIPLYING EXTRAORDINARY PRAYER

- One hour of individual prayer at least five days each week.
- One hour of corporate prayer with the group each week.
- Four-hour extended prayer time at least once per month (half night or all night).

Note: These goals are just recommended starting places. Many of our teams pray much more than this from the beginning, and all of our teams continue to grow in prayer.[7]

Chapter 14

Go Out Among the Lost

The third element in "raising the sails" for movement is "Go Out Among the Lost."

When people talk about Church Planting Movements and the DMM strategy, they're talking about movements that reach lost people. Movements are all about lost people becoming disciples of Jesus and gathering in churches, then making more disciples of Jesus.

There is no movement unless lost people are becoming disciples. Naturally, then, you have to "go out among the lost" to see movements start. That requires leaving the church building and doing what Jesus told his disciples to do in Matthew 10 and Luke 10. I explained the process briefly in chapter 5.

> *You have to "go out among the lost" to see movements start.*

Going out is a difficult step for most Christians. We're used to going to church, going home, and going back again next weekend. We're used to hanging out mostly around Christians. We're used to the holy huddle. But lost people won't be reached that way. We've got to break out of our Christian bubble and take seriously Jesus' command to "go and make disciples of all the nations" (Matthew 28:18–20)! Let me give you an example of how this looks.

An often-repeated DMM principle is, "Expect the hardest places to yield the greatest results." Therefore, in our desire to reach the million, we wanted to start in the hardest places.

> *"Expect the hardest places to yield the greatest results."*

Inspired by Steve Addison's book *What Jesus Started*, I contacted a friend of mine who was a Lubbock police officer and asked, "What neighborhoods are known to be the most dangerous in the city? Can you give me the top three?"[1] He gave me the top three most dangerous neighborhoods, and several of our DMM churches decided to target them as they went out among the lost. We started prayer walking one of those difficult neighborhoods every week. We asked that God would allow us to meet and serve people as we walked. We also asked that God would lead us to the person of peace (Matthew 10; Luke 10) who was open to the gospel and prepared to help that neighborhood receive it.

As we walked, we would talk to people who were outside. We would tell them we were prayer walking the neighborhood; then we'd ask if they had anything about which we could pray for them. People are generally receptive to being prayed for, so we were able to serve many people in that way. This first step helps to determine if they are open spiritually.

Over time, in the first neighborhood, God allowed us to meet Randy. He invited us into his home, and we were able to spend time talking to him about his needs. He shared that he really wanted to be a better spiritual leader for his family.

Ding, ding, ding! There was our open door.

As we began to talk about spiritual things, Randy

mentioned that he was considering taking his kids back to church (even though neither he nor his kids enjoyed going). We told him that "going to church" is a good thing but that we felt like we could offer him something that would help even more.

We knew that if we could get a Discovery Group started with Randy and his family, they might all come to Christ together, plant a new church, and then become effective disciple makers and church planters, which would lead to many more churches being planted in that area. That would be a lot more fruitful than just telling Randy to go back to a church he didn't enjoy and attend services each weekend.

We told Randy that we believed we could meet some of his needs and that we wanted to meet with him again. As we prepared to leave Randy's home, we prayed with him that God would do a miracle in his life.

After our first meeting with Randy, we kept our word. We helped him find a good attorney and also helped him find better housing options. That very week, once his needs were met, we set up a time to meet again.

As we prepare to go out among the lost, we pray first and ask the Lord where he wants us to go. Once he gives us direction, we begin prayer walking that place. We look for opportunities to meet needs, and we share about Jesus! Just like what happened with Randy.

When Stan first talked to us about "going out among the lost," we asked him, "Shouldn't we start first with the people in our relational network who are lost?" He said that while we don't want to neglect our relational network, if we wait to "go out among the lost" until we've shared with family and friends, we'll inadvertently train ourselves *not* to "go out among the lost." In other words, we won't be in the habit of going out each week. Plus, he said, we'll run out of family and friends to talk to quickly anyway.

> When you go out among the lost, your ultimate goal is to find the person of peace.

One important thing to remember, and this is what makes the DMM strategy a little different from what most of us are used to, when you go out among the lost, your ultimate goal is to find the person of peace Jesus spoke about in Matthew 10 and Luke 10. You're looking for the receptive person whom God has prepared to be a bridge for the gospel to travel over into that community.

Stan shared with us a helpful acronym to identify "persons of peace" using the characteristics listed in Matthew 10 and Luke 10. The acronym is WOOLY.

W stands for *Welcoming*. Persons of peace are those who are welcoming. They are open and receptive to you and your message. When you ask to pray for them, they respond positively. When you start a spiritual conversation with them, they are open to discussing spiritual things. When you serve him or her, your act of service is received well. See Luke 10:5–8.

OO stands for *Open Oikos*. *Oikos* is a Greek word that is used in these passages. It is often translated "house" or "household" and carries the idea of those closest to you—people in your relational network who are very close to you, such as your immediate family and even your very close friends. Persons of peace are those who "open their oikos" to the message. That means they're willing to gather their close friends and family together to hear and respond to the message. Typically, we'll ask someone, "Would you like to bring your family and friends together to discover more about God through his Word?" We call these groups of people who gather together Discovery Groups (DGs). The emphasis is always on bringing a group of people together, rather than focusing on an individual. This was Jesus' pattern, and it was also the pattern in the book of Acts. See Luke 10:5 and Acts 10.

L stands for *Listen.* Persons or households of peace are willing not only to hear the message but to obey it and share it with others. They receive the message as being from God and needing to be obeyed and shared. We encourage them to begin a DG with their family and friends. We train these people to read and retell a passage of Scripture using the seven DBS questions as a guide.[2] Two of those questions deal with obeying and sharing. If, after some period of time, the oikos is obeying and sharing, you've likely found your person or household of peace. If not, this may not be the person or household God has prepared to receive the gospel and bridge it to the community. See Luke 10:8–11 for how to respond based on whether people welcome or reject the message.

Y doesn't actually stand for anything. Adding the final letter just turns WOOL, a noun, into WOOLY to provide an adjective for describing persons of peace.

When we're out among the lost, we're looking for WOOLY people, or persons of peace, whom God has prepared to receive the message and to pass it on to others, just as Jesus did when he sent out his disciples.

GOALS FOR GOING OUT AMONG THE LOST

- Spend at least one hour each week as a team going out among the lost (new areas with people you haven't met).

- Spend time loving, serving, and sharing with your family, friends, coworkers, and neighbors.

Note: These goals are just recommended starting places. Many of our teams spend much more than one hour among the lost each week. Some teams spend five or more hours each week seeking persons of peace among the lost.[3]

Chapter 15

See Groups Start

The fourth element in "raising the sails" for movement is "See Groups Start."

We go out among the lost (third element) with the intention of finding the person of peace who opens up their oikos so a DG can get started and a discipleship process can begin. That's the goal.

The prayer is that as the DG journeys together through a series of "Creation to Christ" Scripture passages, all persons in the group repent of their sin and place their faith in Christ as Lord. We then lead them through getting baptized together and beginning to function as a DMM church. We begin training them immediately to focus on God's Word, multiply extraordinary prayer, go out among the lost, and see groups start so the process can repeat all over again.

Let me continue Randy's story from the previous chapter.

When Randy expressed that he wanted to be a better spiritual leader for his family, we knew this could be an open door. At the very least we felt that he was welcoming (the *W* in WOOLY).

When we met with Randy the second time, after his

immediate needs had been met, I brought up that we could also help him become a better spiritual leader for his family, if he was interested. He definitely was. I asked him, "Would you be open to bringing your family and friends together to discover more about God through his Word?" He said he was and that Sundays were the best days to meet.

Once he told me that Sunday mornings would be a good time for his oikos to meet, I began right then to train him in exactly what to do. I taught him the seven-question DBS method of reading, obeying, and sharing the Word of God. Then I gave him the "Creation to Christ" passages, which he could give his family each week. Then I walked him through a mock Discovery Group so he'd know exactly how to lead it. I told him he could try it that weekend and then we could meet again and discuss any questions he had. I could tell he was excited to begin to lead his family spiritually, and I began to pray that the Holy Spirit would speak through the Word of God and draw all of the family to saving faith in Jesus Christ!

I never attended Randy's group. That's ideal. If the potential person of peace asks us to attend the first few times to help him or her learn the seven-question DBS process, we will do that. But our goal is always to be gone by the fourth week. We want the group to become dependent on the Holy Spirit as the "Bible answer person" or the "leader" rather than any of us. Ideally, the person of peace would be trained ahead of time and coached each week rather than having any of us attend the group. Sometimes the person of peace just wants you to come to help them get started, which is understandable. In this case, Randy was willing to lead without me being there, so I told him I'd train him and then coach him each week through any questions or struggles he had.

The goal in "seeing groups start" is generational growth. Remember, movements are often measured using multiple streams of fourth-generation growth as a guide.

We want to see groups started that start new groups that start more new groups and so on. Randy's DG is generation 1. If a family member

The goal in "seeing groups start" is generational growth.

in Randy's group starts another DG with some neighbors, it would be generation 2. If one of those neighbors started another DG with his or her coworkers, that would be generation 3. If one of those coworkers started another DG with some friends, that would be generation 4, and so on. As we coach the persons of peace to lead the DGs, we're encouraging them to read God's Word, obey it, share it with others, and start new groups. That's how you get generational growth.

Stan had prepared us for the fact that, around the world, most DGs do not become churches. He said it's much like the parable of the farmer scattering seed in Matthew 13:1–23. On a worldwide average, about one in four DGs actually survive. That's why we've got to be out among the lost as much as possible, so we can see as many groups started as possible, so that hopefully 25 percent (or more) become functioning DMM churches.

As you can tell, this takes time.

One of the DMM principles that you'll learn in the DMM training is "go slow to go fast." DMM starts slowly. You're taking Jesus' approach of looking for the person of peace, staying with that person for a while, and trusting that God will use him or her to bring the gospel to the neighborhood and community. Although the process starts slowly, once it gets traction, it can produce rapid multiplication that reaches millions. This

"Go slow to go fast." outpaces population growth frequently in that area as it races toward reaching the entire people group.[1]

GOALS FOR SEEING GROUPS START

- See one DG (Discovery Group) started per person per year.

Note: If there are ten people on the DMM team, they're hoping to see ten DGs started in a given year, which would hopefully lead to planting two new churches each year (based on the 25 percent principle mentioned above).[2]

Chapter 16

Cast Vision

The fifth element in "raising the sails" for movement is "Cast Vision."

DMM researcher and Beyond staff member Justin Long tweeted, "Raising up 1 team of 2 to 3 people can reach 100,000. Be a strategic mobilizer of 100 and you could potentially make a difference for 5 million or more (100/2*100k). This is a critical role."[1]

If you raise up just one team to focus on God's Word, multiply extraordinary prayer, go out among the lost, and see groups start, you can reach a lot of people. But think about how many people you could reach if you raised up multiple teams to do the same thing? One team can be effective, but ten, twenty-five, fifty, or one hundred teams can greatly multiply your effectiveness and can increase the likelihood of reaching your people group. In other words, we cast vision to get more believers involved in disciple making and church planting. The more people who are involved, the more people who can potentially be reached. Let me give a practical example of how we've done this with the people we trained through eLife.

Nine months prior to our ten-year anniversary, we started

> *The more people who are involved, the more people who can potentially be reached.*

casting vision to people in our church whom we thought might be interested in participating in DMM training. About one hundred people expressed interest in being trained to make disciples and plant churches.

We then spent the next several months taking those people through the training. During the last lesson we encouraged them to cast vision to family, friends, coworkers, and neighbors who might be interested in going through the training. We asked them to contact on-fire believers and ask them if they'd be interested in being trained to be disciple makers and church planters too. Some of them called their friends to talk to them about it individually. Others took people to lunch to explain more about what they were doing. Still others sat down with their entire family and asked if anyone wanted to take part. We then told them that these people could possibly become part of their DMM church planting team once they were trained. That's how we formed the DMM church planting teams that we have today.

The more vision we cast to others, the more people we'll be able to train. The more people we train, the more teams that will form. The more teams that form, the more people we have the potential to reach. That's why the Casting Vision element is so important.

We encourage all DMM practitioners to continue to cast vision to their believing friends about what God is doing through their disciple-making efforts. We're hoping to inspire as many believers as possible to consider becoming disciple makers and church planters so one million people can be reached for Christ.

One of the great tragedies of the American church model, and it's happened at our church too, is an attitude that results in suppressing the gifts, ambitions, and callings of ordinary believers. This attitude seems to suggest that ordinary people are supposed to just sit in church and watch while the real professionals do the work of the ministry. The average churchgoer's main job is to make sure he or she comes back to services next weekend and funds the buildings, programs, and salaries. Of course, we wouldn't ever *say* this, but that's how it comes across. I believe Jesus intended the Great Commission in Matthew 28 to be for every believer, not just pastors and church staff members. Yet, because of the way we "do" church, most believers think that disciple making and church planting fall on the pastor's shoulders alone.

Churchgoers don't typically hear the term *disciple maker* and think, *That's me!* And they definitely don't hear the term *church planter* and think, *That's me!* Many aren't sure if they can even do those things. Many have assumed those are the jobs of the pastors.

I definitely don't think this is how Jesus intended it to be.

Casting the vision to American Christians of being disciple makers and church planters is definitely an uphill battle, since change comes hard. We as pastors and leaders haven't done a very good job of training people to think of themselves as disciple makers or church planters. And yet the prevalent way of thinking in DMM is that "average" Christians are, by definition, disciple makers and church planters.

We've got to keep casting vision to American Christians that God can use them in the same way. God's great purpose for the American Christian is not just that they'd go to church each week, listen to a sermon, go home, and then go back again the next weekend. No way.

If we're going to reach our people group and see millions come to Christ, ordinary Christians have to be empowered to believe God wants to use them to make disciples and plant churches! A lot of deconstruction will likely have to take place in an American Christian's mind to really believe this, but it's worth the effort in casting vision.

A great example comes from one of eLife's DMM Church Planters. We cast vision to him, trained him, and then sent him out to train his team. Once he trained the team, he and his team left our church and began to function as a DMM church planting team. I asked him later how it was going. He said, "I feel like we were set free."

I was shocked at this answer. And it hurt a little. We definitely weren't trying to hold people in bondage while they were coming to our church. Much of what the American church does to people is unintentional, I'm sure. I had to wonder why he felt "set free" when we laid hands on him and sent him out with his team. Then I realized it was likely because, for the first time in his life, someone was saying to him, "*You* can do this! You don't have to wait for your pastor to make disciples. You don't have to just sit in a pew and hope your pastor plants churches. God wants to use *you*!"

This person definitely didn't mean for that phrase to affect me the way it did, but I was so convicted. We never wanted to enslave people to our church. We didn't want to keep people in bondage to our ministries. We wanted people to feel that they could hear from the Lord and do whatever he told them to do! We wanted people not just to attend the church we planted; we wanted them to make disciples and plant many of their own churches.

I decided from that day forward that I'd set as many

people free as I could. I never again wanted our church or me to be the reason people believed God couldn't use them to make many disciples and start many churches. Filling up a room was no longer my measure of success.

We realized that if we want to partner with other churches and organizations to see a million people reached in the next ten years, and if we want to to see our whole people group reached in the next twenty years, we had to start casting vision like crazy. American pastors have to set the Christians in their churches free. We've got to recover the "culture of empowerment" of ordinary believers that was evident in the first-century church. Did you know that leaders of the movement in India that has reached millions point to this same "culture of empowerment" as being essential to movement? We've got to empower ordinary people once again. Remember this verse: "The members of the council were amazed when they saw the boldness of Peter and John, for they could see that they were ordinary men with no special training in the Scriptures. They also recognized them as men who had been with Jesus" (Acts 4:13).

God loves using "ordinary men [and women] with no special training in the Scriptures" who have "been with Jesus." We've got to set the Peters and Johns free! Pastors and leaders, I implore you to join me in *setting them free*!

GOALS FOR CASTING VISION

- Cast vision to one believer each week to be a part of an upcoming DMM training.[2]

Chapter 17

Train Believers

The sixth element in "raising the sails" for movement is "Train Believers."

After casting vision to people to be generational disciple makers and church planters, we need to train them! And what are we training them to do? Go out among the lost and see groups start! The same thing we've been doing!

We're training them to make disciples and plant churches. And, more specifically, we're training them to make disciples who make more disciples who make more disciples, hopefully leading to multiple streams of disciples made down to the fourth generation and beyond.

In chapter 10, I explained more about the training we offer to those who are interested. It's the same training that has catalyzed many movements all over the world. And it's the same training that Stan gave us at the very beginning of this journey. This training is twelve lessons, derived from various Scripture passages on disciple making.

The length of time it takes to complete the lessons varies. A traditional American Bible study would take twelve weeks, because participants would do one lesson each week. But remember, we are concerned with obedience, not just knowledge acquisition.

As I mentioned previously, I often describe the training as "biblical principles to be obeyed, not information to be transferred." As a result, you might spend two weeks just trying to obey lesson 1. Or it might take you three weeks to get through lesson 6 as you're trying to obey the biblical principles in that lesson.

The goal is that by the time you finish the twelfth lesson, you're obeying all of the Scripture passages you read in the training. When I went through the training, I was surprised by how much I hadn't been *obeying*. I should've been, but I wasn't. I had learned it. I had memorized it. I had been in many Bible studies about it. But I hadn't obeyed it. Obedience is what changes everything.

> *I was surprised by how much I hadn't been obeying.*

The reason we spend time casting vision and training believers is because the more teams we have "raising the sails," the more disciples we'll likely make and the more churches we'll likely plant. So, while we're going out among the lost and seeing groups start, we want to be training others simultaneously to do the same.

The reason we gave our DMM churches a goal of casting vision to one person per week is because we're assuming it will take casting vision to thirty people to find ten who are willing to go through the training. If you start with one person per week in January, thirty weeks later is approximately midsummer. Hopefully, by midsummer, you've cast vision to thirty people and have found ten who are willing to be trained. Then you can start the ten-person DMM training in August or September and hopefully finish it by the end of the year, since it usually takes three to five months to complete.

My DMM coach says constantly that Church Planting Movements are basically Training Movements. Training is vital for rapid exponential growth because new leaders are constantly being raised up.

And remember, training doesn't mean teaching people a lot of information. Training is done best through what we call the MAWL approach: MAWL = Model. Assist. Watch. Launch.

A great example of MAWL is learning to drive a stick shift vehicle. When I turned sixteen, my dad bought an old truck for me. The only problem was that it wasn't an automatic; it was a stick shift, and I had no idea how to drive it.

Training is done best through the MAWL approach: Model. Assist. Watch. Launch.

Dad took me out to a shopping mall in town with a big parking lot, and he began to teach me. First, he "modeled" it. He had me watch him drive. Next, he put me in the driver's seat, and he "assisted" me in doing it. I would push down on the clutch, and he would change the gears for me. Then I began to change the gears. At that point, he would just "watch" me and instruct me as I did it. Then, after a while (and it took a long while for me to get the hang of it), he was able to "launch" me to do it on my own.

That's what we mean by "training." If my father had simply sat me down in our living room and given me a lecture on how to drive a stick shift, I never would've been able to do it. A lecture doesn't help you learn to drive a stick shift. You've got to have someone get in the car and train you by using the MAWL method. Lectures aren't designed to teach

Lectures aren't designed to teach you to obey.

you to obey; they're designed to transfer information into your brain.

DMM training is "on the job" training, and you're many times going out and applying it along with your team. It's not lecture oriented. Often you'll observe your trainer modeling a principle, then the trainer will assist you in applying it. He or she will then watch you apply it on your own, then will launch you to apply it on your own from then on. This type of training ensures that you're obeying and applying, not just learning.

GOALS FOR TRAINING BELIEVERS

- Lead at least one training each year with the people to whom you've cast vision.[1]

Chapter 18

Ongoing Coaching

The seventh and final element in "raising the sails" for movement is "Ongoing Coaching." I've already written in chapter 9 on the importance of this element, but there's more great details to cover.

As I've looked for coaches in the past to help me with starting a church, or to help me with the transition to DMM, or even to help me with businesses I've started, I've looked for someone who has experienced the same results I want to experience. There are a lot of theorists out there; and while some of them may make great coaches, I've always been helped most by people who have already been where I'm wanting to go—people who have already seen what I'm hoping to see. These people can speak from having "been there, done that," rather than guess based on what they think *might* work. This seemed especially important as I started looking for coaches who could help our church with our 1,000,000 in 10 years vision. I knew I wanted coaches who had seen millions come to Christ!

I knew immediately that I had to look outside of America. I don't know any pastor or leader in the States who has seen a million disciples made in fifty years, much less ten years. The largest American churches have reached people in the tens of thousands, but I've never heard of any movement in America in modern times that has seen millions.

Missiologists who study movements agree.

I get a monthly email from a movements researcher who documents where movements have been catalyzed around the world. The last time I looked, there were only two, maybe three, movements documented in America. The one that we know of for sure has disciples numbering more than one hundred thousand and growing, but not quite in the millions yet. And, believe it or not, this movement wasn't even started out of a church. Rather, it was started out of a nonprofit that ministers to the poor. Our Leadership Team has visited this ministry, and we were astounded by the tens of thousands of disciples who have come to faith in Jesus through them.

Looking outside of America for a few coaches led me to my primary DMM coach, Stan, who lives in Dubai in the United Arab Emirates and a leader from India whose name I'll omit for security reasons but whose story I mentioned in chapter 4. Both of these people have been a part of movements that have reached millions.

To me, another great tragedy in the American church is that it seems many American pastors, including myself for a long time, aren't even aware that millions are being reached overseas. If we were, perhaps we'd reach out to some of these leaders and invite them to coach, mentor, and train us so that we might pray and strategize toward a similar movement of God in our country. However, since we're often not aware of what's happening in the larger world, American pastors usually choose other American pastors as coaches and mentors.

There's nothing inherently wrong with that, but you'll likely only experience what those American pastors have experienced, because you'll do the same things they have done. With some influence from overseas, where these movements are bringing millions to Christ, we might be able to identify problems in the American church that act as barriers to our experiencing a great movement of God.

Harry Brown, in his foreword of *The Kingdom Unleashed*, said,

> *American pastors usually choose other American pastors as coaches and mentors.*

> The Global North [North America and Europe] has much to be proud of in what it has accomplished in the last two centuries of missionary work. But the cold, hard reality is that we have pretty much found the ceiling on what can be accomplished with the approaches we are using. By contrast, what God is doing through His people in the Global South [Asia, Africa, and Latin America] is creating an upheaval that is tossing the status quo out the window. A timeless truth states, "The humble get better." It is time for all of us on this half of the globe to listen and learn from the folks on the other side.[1]

Our church is still in the very early stages of implementing a DMM strategy, but we wouldn't have had a clue how to even get started without coaching from overseas. Much of what they're doing there to reach millions is totally foreign to the American church. I've had to do a lot of deconstruction in my own mind to be able to even understand what my coaches and those involved in movements abroad are saying to me. The way they view church and discipleship is so different from the way they are viewed in America. And as I hear them talk about it, if I'm being honest, their view aligns so much more with what I've read in Scripture than what I had always been taught to do as an American church pastor.

We wouldn't have had a clue how to even get started without coaching from overseas.

I call my coaches constantly and ask questions. I share with them what we're doing and ask for feedback. I pass along their wisdom to our Leadership Team and we try to implement their ideas here. We want to "raise the sails" here in the same way they've "raised the sails" in their countries, so that we might see in America what they've seen where they are, if the Holy Spirit chooses to "blow on our sails"!

I can't stress enough the importance of having a coach if you're going to dive into DMM. You need someone to take you through the initial DMM training. Then you need someone to guide you as you implement what you learn. You need someone to whom you can ask questions and someone who will help you troubleshoot difficulties along the way. My coaches have been an incredible resource in all of these situations.

My DMM coach told me that in these movements it's common to meet with a coach at least weekly in your first two to three years. You need to have that much input. The coaches often use as a model the three years that Jesus spent with his disciples.

Each of our teams that have been sent out from eLife meets with one of our leaders weekly for coaching. We talk about how their implementation of the seven elements went that week and what they can improve for the next week. We tell powerful stories, and we pray for each other that we would see many disciples made and many churches planted. I encourage you, if you're interested in getting started in DMM, to reach out to us. We can pair you with a DMM coach who can conduct your training and then guide you along as you begin to implement the principles. Roy Moran said, "Movements live and die on good mentoring and coaching."[2]

GOALS FOR ONGOING COACHING

- Participate in an Ongoing Coaching meeting at least once per week.[3]

Chapter 19

Akachi

One of my DMM coaches and author of *Spent Matches*, Roy Moran, posted this picture on Facebook recently.[1]

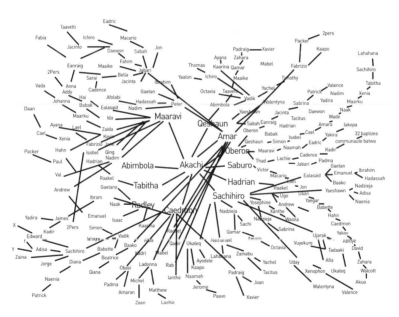

The caption was, "What is DMM (Disciple Making Movement)? Here is a picture of one man's life from East Africa."

Someone said once that a picture is worth a thousand words, and that's definitely true here.

A man named Akachi wanted to obey Jesus and begin making disciples. As a result, he began sharing with Oberon. Since Akachi was trained in DMM principles, he likely would've been sharing with Oberon and his entire oikos. Through his conversations with Akachi, Oberon was undoubtedly transformed by Jesus, and he began to share with Qeshaun and his entire oikos. Qeshaun met Jesus and began to share with Simon, who began to share with Isabel, who began to share with Cael, who began to share with another Amara, who began to share with Wade, who began to share with Naak, who began to share with Maarku, who began to share with Xenia, who began to share with Tabitha, who began to share with Sachihiro, who began to share with Lahahana.

In that one stream alone, thirteen generations were impacted! *Thirteen!* And it all started with Akachi listening to Jesus and beginning to make disciples who would make more disciples. This is a prime example of generational discipleship that is catalyzing movements of God all over the world.

Because of the extraordinary impact the picture Roy posted had on me, I shared it with our staff. Stan, who was also familiar with the story, chimed in, saying, "For the diagram above, this leader talked about trying and failing in DMM and having to go back and rework and reexamine everything he was doing and start all over. God has used them to reach seventeen generations!"

Akachi got excited about DMM and initially failed in implementing it. He didn't give up—he started over again and now has reached up to seventeen generations in East Africa.

I don't know about you, but this fires me up.

I want to be like Akachi; don't you? I want to obey Jesus and make disciples generationally the way he did; don't you?

I want to be like Akachi; don't you?

What's stopping us? We can begin today! Even if you've tried and failed, you can start over. Just as Akachi did.

Lord, use us to make disciples in our country as you used Akachi to make disciples in his!

Chapter 20

Andrew and Kristin

Kristin and her husband, Andrew, are some of eLife's most effective disciple makers. They went through the first round of DMM training in the spring of 2017; we commissioned them and sent them out as church planters at our ten-year anniversary. As of this book's publication, they and their team have started several first-generation Discovery Groups, and they've even seen one second-generation Discovery Group started—and all of this in just six months or so.

Here is Kristin's story in her own words:

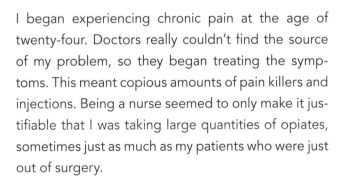

I began experiencing chronic pain at the age of twenty-four. Doctors really couldn't find the source of my problem, so they began treating the symptoms. This meant copious amounts of pain killers and injections. Being a nurse seemed to only make it justifiable that I was taking large quantities of opiates, sometimes just as much as my patients who were just out of surgery.

But there was never really enough to get rid of my pain totally; and, honestly, I felt entitled to live a pain-free life. I felt it was a basic human right.

I started to notice how much wastage of narcotics was being thrown away. Wastage is what is left over in a vial after the nurse pulls up the prescribed amount for the patient. The rest just gets thrown away. It really didn't seem to me that I was hurting anyone by taking this wastage home with me. I wasn't taking anything away from anyone; it was just trash, after all.

Unfortunately, this isn't how the DEA saw it. After six years of flying under the radar of everyone, even my own family, my addiction became too strong, and I started making mistakes that eventually led to me losing it all. I lost my husband, my nursing license, my kids, and my freedom.

After the DEA told me they were issuing a warrant for a felony (fraudulently obtaining a controlled substance), I decided to try and get some money together to hire an attorney, but no one would hire me. I couldn't turn to my family because they had pretty much received the shock of their lives and deemed me beyond help.

I met a guy in a bar one night who showed me how to make a profit selling weed. I took that knowledge and began to try and make it work. I was pretty successful; but in that lifestyle, run-ins with the law are inevitable. My felony warrant caught up with me, and I found myself in Lubbock County Detention Center waiting for my court-appointed lawyer to get me a fair trial.

The reality was very different. I broke down and took the first plea I was offered just so I could be out quicker. With no money on your books, county is a hard place to survive. While incarcerated my landlord sold all my belongings in lieu of rent I owed, my ex-husband sent me divorce papers and took full custody of our children, and I got out with my car and the clothes on my back.

I really tried to get it right, but no one would give me a chance after they found out I was on felony probation. I turned back to what I knew worked. But this time I did it with a broken spirit; I felt unloved and completely alone. I started doing more and more drugs.

I met my now husband in a trap house. We were both there doing drugs, and I had an instant attraction to him. It was deeper than physical for me; I could see his brokenness too. We began spending every day together, and I eventually asked him if I could squat with him in his mom's old abandoned house. He said, "Sure," so we cleaned out a spot to sleep and made it ours. We had electricity but no water.

He encouraged me to get off the hard drugs, and I desperately wanted to, but the pain in my back was coming back fiercely. I found myself in the ER having trouble lifting my right leg, along with severe pain in my upper back. The doctors wrote it off as a pulled ligament. They gave me muscle relaxers and didn't even take an X-ray.

Three days later I woke up paralyzed from my T4

vertebra down. As a nurse I knew I was in pretty bad shape, as I had lost complete usage of my bowels and bladder. Usually complete loss to this point is a good indication of damage too severe to fix. The doctors at the ER had a hard time believing that I just woke up like this; but after the MRI showed a blockage of some sort on my spinal cord, they took me back for emergency surgery.

After waking up I was still unable to move. The doctors told my family my condition was permanent, and they needed to start to think about who I would live with. Unfortunately for me, no one was offering.

The doctors decided to place me in a nursing home for "rehab," but I knew how this worked. I'd been a nurse for ten years and a CNA for four years before that. I had worked in several nursing homes, so I knew that this was where I would likely live out my remaining days.

The reality of my situation began to hit me hard the first night I was there. I was crying and sobbing uncontrollably. I couldn't believe this was my life now. After the CNA came in to change my soiled bed that I had an accident on, I was at a breaking point. I began to cry out to God. I said, "God, I'm so sorry for all the bad I've done, and I know I deserve this; but if you are real and Jesus died for me because of love, then please love me enough to just give me the strength to get through this because I'd rather die than live like this."

I never expected a miracle—just the strength to come to terms with my new reality. But that next morning I was filled with a sense of peace and a desire to walk again, knowing that I could. So I borrowed my roommate's walker and stood for the first time.

All sadness and self-pity had left me, and now I had strength and hope. The nursing home had no desire to start me on physical therapy, so I had to push them. In the meantime, I began to use the old abandoned therapy room there in the facility. I would literally drag my legs behind me on the parallel bars until they started to cooperate. I found out early on that I had to get over my fear of falling because I was going to fall a lot! I finally had therapy the last two weeks of my stay there, but I was already walking when I got to therapy.

I had also paid a visit to a judge after my probation officer revoked me. The judge deemed me medically unfit for prison, so he gave me time served on the remainder of my four years.

Miracles were happening in my life, but I was still too blind to see.

A pivotal moment for me was when I went to see my neurosurgeon at my six-week post-op visit. He was so astounded to see me walking that he took me into the lobby and called the other doctors who had worked on my case to watch me walk across the room. Then he took me back to his office and told me that medically and scientifically speaking, my walking was not possible. He said, "This is a miracle, a true gift from God. I'd hate for you to think that this was because of me or because of you. This is the work of God, and I had twenty cases like yours of people this year who would give anything to be in your shoes. Do not waste this gift."

I did not know how to process this. I mean, I did cry out to God, but why would he listen to me? I was a horrible sinner and a complete failure. I'd been a star player on the wrong team for years.

I left the nursing home walking just thirty days later and went back to live with my boyfriend. We went back to selling drugs, but something was changing in my heart. I wanted to find out more about why God would choose me for a miracle, and I wanted to know why I had the cyst develop on my spinal cord in the first place.

I ended up finding a comorbid disease called Arnold Chiari malformation that fit the symptoms of my life perfectly. I'd always suffered migraines and dizziness and pain for no apparent reason. So I had my doctor check me for it, and sure enough, I had it. I also made a bargain with my boyfriend that if I was able to get on disability, we would never use any of that money to sell drugs. He reluctantly agreed, and it was a long three-year battle, but eventually it happened. No more struggling for a place to live; we could now rent an apartment.

Shortly after I found out I would need brain surgery, I found out I was pregnant. I told Andrew that I really wanted to try and get my life back on track and get my kids back. He got a job, but I could tell he was not fully in support of my new lifestyle ideas. After our daughter was born, I had brain surgery, but there was an issue. The patch they used to cover my brain was failing, and all of my cerebral spinal fluid was leaking out and forming a large pocket of fluid under my scalp. I felt so ill; I was convinced that I was dying, and I had just a few months before regaining primary custody of my kids.

Desperate, we drove across country to see a specialist who was supposed to save my life, but after seeing my MRI he refused to help me because I was a liability. Disappointed, we drove back, but on the trip I began to recall all the things I'd already gone through and how Jesus had healed me against all odds before. So I told Andy I was done with doctors, and I was giving this up to God. Once again I started to see God move miraculously. I began to feel much better and even noticed the grapefruit-sized lump at my surgery site was shrinking.

I was awake early one Sunday morning when I saw a sermon on TV. It was like the pastor was speaking directly to me. So I decided to set my alarm and start having church there every Sunday morning with my family. My husband thought it was just a phase and I'd soon be over this whole God thing. He got up willingly the first few weeks, but then it became a struggle.

So I gave him an ultimatum. I said, "God has healed me twice and answered my cries in the darkest hours of my life, and I want to explore him more. You are either with me or against me, but if you are against me, you can't live here anymore."

I had a parent-teacher conference scheduled

that week. I began telling my daughter's teacher all about my journey, and she invited me to her church. When she said it was Experience Life, I said I watched that on TV every Sunday. I had no idea it was here in Lubbock; I just thought it was broadcast from Dallas or something. She said, "No, it's here," and I agreed to go visit the actual church one day.

I was still too weak. But soon my strength was coming back, and after we moved into our new duplex, we decided to check out the Downtown Campus. I felt God moving there! I gave my life to Christ that first time and began going back every week. But I felt like I wasn't getting enough from just Sundays and Wednesday Night Prayer. I needed more, so I began reading my Bible. In less than a year, I read the entire book. But, still, every time I opened it there was something new and unexpected grabbing hold of my heart. I read a scripture in Romans that changed things for me. "Because of the weakness of your human nature, I am using the illustration of slavery to help you understand all this. Previously, you let yourselves be slaves to impurity and lawlessness, which led ever deeper into sin. Now you must give yourselves to be slaves to righteous living so that you will become holy" (6:19).

I decided to be all in for God. I started doing the Next Steps.[1] I got baptized, joined a LifeTransformation Group, started volunteering, and my now husband and I decided to abstain until we got married. The wedding was a few weeks later. No, I'm kidding. It was a few months later, but it seemed like forever! We also decided to start saying yes to God and stop making excuses.

We took Perspectives, and that really changed the game for us.[2] We previously had little understanding of the Great Commission, but this course opened our eyes. We not only found our calling but everyone's calling. Jesus left standing orders for every one of his followers, and we were not only unaware of this calling, but we were not doing it at all.

After Perspectives we did a Phase One Goer Group and learned how we could affect the nations right here in Lubbock.[3] We wanted desperately to go on a mission trip and just last year went to Thailand. I could not prepare my heart for what I experienced there. I could only imagine my daughter knowing the way to heaven but keeping it a secret from her brother. How come it's 2018 and there are people in this world who still don't know about Jesus? Didn't he say go tell everyone? What have we as a church been doing?

I got involved in reaching out to international students here in Lubbock, but I started to notice that the lost are here too. And if we are training up believers to go out and make disciples who are doing the same, the chances of places like Thailand being reached become greater. How can I go to the grocery store every day and just do my business without looking up to see the despair in the hearts of those all around me?

God began to break my heart for his children. I want to tell them all about what he's done for me, how he's a good Father and how his love abounds and how he heals and how Jesus is the way, but I didn't know exactly how to do it.

When I heard about the DMM training, I knew it was something my heart had been crying out for. I didn't hesitate! After the training I knew it would be hard to break free from the comfort of Sunday morning church that had fostered me so well; but it was a smooth transition, and now my Sunday is just as full! We meet together, worship, offer support and encouragement; and then, just like the original group of misfit apostles, we go out and try to pray for people. We try to see God do miracles like healing the sick and reach out to people to start Discovery Groups so they can see God's Word come to fullness in their own lives.

Saying yes to God never turns out wrong, I promise you! It was his yes to me that made me walk; it was his yes to me that healed my brain; and as impactful as those yeses were, nothing compared to when I said yes to him!

Jesus said yes on the cross, and if he was willing, so should I be. I want everyone to know that no matter how unloved and unworthy you feel, God still loves you, and if you are willing He will use you.

Surrendering to Jesus was the best decision I've ever made, and praying for God to use me has been the most powerful prayer I've ever prayed. If I tried this in my own strength, I'd fail. It's only by his strength, by his grace, and it is all for his glory.[4]

In a recent coaching meeting I talked to Andrew and Kristin about going out among the lost and looking for persons of peace. What they told me blew me away. They said they've been going to Walmart twice a week to pray for people. They didn't give many more details than that, so I started to probe and ask more questions.

I asked them if those two weekly trips to Walmart are specifically to get groceries and if they just happen to pray for people while they are there. They said that they do their personal shopping at other times and that the two weekly trips they mentioned are times they go with the sole intent to pray with people and try to find persons of peace.

I was surprised to hear that they go to Walmart a few extra times each week just to talk to people. I asked them how long they typically stay there praying for people. They told me they stay about two to three hours each time.

I almost fell out of my chair.

Let me remind you that Andrew and Kristin aren't full-time pastors. They are ordinary people . . . with full-time jobs.

I asked Andrew and Kristin how many people they can pray for in a two- to three-hour period. They said they typically pray for forty-five people before they leave and that they've taught their daughter to pray for people too. With her help, it is easier to get to the forty-five.

I started laughing out loud! I was thinking, *Who do they think they are, disciple makers of Jesus or something?* I asked them what they say when they walk up to people, imagining those interactions are a bit awkward. They said that they just greet people at random and let them know that they are out praying for people. Next, they ask if they can pray for the person in some way.

I asked them about the response they usually receive. They said that almost everyone responds positively and wants prayer. They told me that having gone through the DMM training, one thing they now ask people after they pray for them is, "Would you be interested in getting your family and friends together to discover more from the Bible about God and his plan for your life?"

I then asked how most people had responded to this question. Andrew said they have only started asking that question recently, but many say they'd love to. Then they exchange phone numbers.

I asked Andrew and Kristin what inspired them to start going to Walmart. They said that Phase One was really instrumental in getting them out among the lost and that DMM training helped them see their time among the lost as an opportunity to find persons of peace and start Discovery Groups.

Andrew also said that he and Kristin try to take people with them as often as they can so they can train their friends to do this as well. Andrew said he'll say to his friend, "Here, watch me do it, then you can do it next." He said his friends are usually pretty nervous; but after they see him do it a few times, they're usually open to trying it.

Andrew and Kristin then said another thing I absolutely loved. They said that usually when they pray for people, those people start crying. They said it happens almost every time.

That made so much sense to me. Most people probably aren't used to being prayed for, and when they hear someone start talking to God on their behalf, it is so powerful that they can't help but cry.

Kristin said that their friends think they're crazy, not only because they like to go out "fishing for people" (Matthew 4:19) at Walmart, but also because of how often they go to all-night prayer meetings. She said they just tell their friends that it's not that crazy; they used to stay out all night doing sinful things, so why wouldn't they stay out all night to pray to Jesus now that they're his followers? She tells friends that the Walmart visits aren't crazy either. They used to talk to strangers all the time about selling drugs to them, so why wouldn't they talk now to people all the time about Jesus and offer to pray for them?

Andrew and Kristin are not paid pastors. They are ordinary people who are fired up about Jesus; motivated by the Holy Spirit; trying to obey everything they read in God's Word; trying to share with everyone they can; and trying to make disciples who make disciples and plant churches that plant churches. Can you think of anything more powerful?

Fired-up believers like Andrew and Kristin are an inspiration. As more of us join them, "raising the sails" for movement, 1,000,000 new disciples in 10 years doesn't seem like such a far reach.

Chapter 21

From Microsoft to Ministry

I want to take you back to the very beginning.
While it seems that chapter 1 might have been the beginning of the story, we all know that there is *always* a story behind the story. And that backstory can be just as important as the main story. After all, our backstories often lay the foundation for what's to come. So here is my backstory.

When I was a teenager, I was obsessed with computers. Hardware, software, programming, network administration—you name it, and I was probably into it. I spent hours every day on the computer.

When I was fourteen, I got my first summer job in the technical support department of a local internet service provider called HubNet. I began to pursue Microsoft certifications; I was given the Microsoft Certified Professional (MCP) designation at the age of fifteen and the Microsoft Certified Systems Engineer (MCSE) designation at sixteen. I did some subcontract work for Microsoft through a local company during that time as well. I moved from there to CleanWeb, another Internet service provider that provided filtered internet for families. I was one of CleanWeb's network administrators through much of my time in high school. From about twelve to sixteen years old, I wasn't following Jesus closely. I was passionate about computers, not the things of God. I wasn't just coding and doing network administration; I was living in sin and keeping things from my parents that I was doing online. It was a dark period in my life.

In the meantime, during the same period, something had changed in my dad's life. He was a different man. All of a sudden he wasn't just a churchgoer; he was on fire for God. Dad read his Bible, prayed, and talked about Jesus all the time. When I'd wake up early for school and go downstairs, I'd find him prostrate on the ground praying. I'd ask how long he'd been praying, and usually he'd been lying there two to three hours.

Now, we had always gone as a family to church; but as you know, there's a difference between just going to church and being on fire for God. The church we attended at the time, Indiana Avenue Baptist Church, had offered a class based on a study by Henry Blackaby called *Experiencing God*, and my dad decided to participate.[1] Learning that God wants us to "experience" a love relationship with him and not just "know" about him was life changing for my dad. And our whole family knew it.

I remember one day when I was fifteen or sixteen, my dad came up to my room and asked if he could talk with me for a second. Of course I was busy doing something on the computer, but I paused to talk to him.

Dad knelt next to my bed, opened his *Experiencing God Day-by-Day* devotional, and said, "Son, can I tell you how I've been praying for you?"[2]

Nervous about what was to come, I replied slowly, "Sure."

Dad's eyes filled with tears. He said, "Son, I've been praying that you'd be as passionate about following Jesus as you are about that computer."

That one sentence pierced my heart. Suddenly it became clear to me that I was on the wrong track. In an instant I knew the computer was the "false god" that I worshiped and that I had forsaken the true and living God! I was deeply convicted and even found myself weeping at times knowing that I had sinned greatly against God.

Soon after that, my dad approached me again and let me know that there was a youth edition of *Experiencing God*. He asked, "Would you like to go through it together?"

The Lord had prepared my heart. I wanted to follow him again. I eagerly said yes, and my dad and I began the study together.

Over a nine-week period we went lesson by lesson through *Experiencing God*, and God did in my life through that study what he had done in my dad's. I caught a fire for God that hasn't gone out since. Just like my dad, I realized that God wanted me to experience a love relationship with him and not to just live my life knowing about him but not ever experiencing him. I now see this as the pivotal moment when I learned (and began to appreciate) the difference between knowledge-based discipleship and obedience- or experience-based discipleship.

I became deeply involved in the youth group at our church. To be clear, it wasn't because I had to; no one was forcing me. I really *wanted* to. When our youth worship leader moved on, God put on my heart to learn to play the guitar so I could begin leading worship. Soon after, as my guitar skills improved, I became one of the youth worship leaders.

After graduating from high school, I became involved in the college ministry at our church and became the worship leader for the college group as well. Then I became the associate college pastor, serving under the college pastor, Russ Murphy, who inspired me greatly. Not only did he teach me how to be a better worship leader, but he also taught me how to put together a worship service and even how to preach. Soon I preached my first sermon in the college ministry of Indiana Avenue Baptist Church. I started feeling that God was leading me away from the computer industry and into full-time ministry.

After Russ left Indiana Avenue Baptist Church to move to Nashville, I put my name in the hat to become the next college pastor. That wasn't the Lord's plan for me, as the church was looking for someone with a seminary degree, and I hadn't been to seminary yet.

While I was disappointed at the time, I still felt a leading into full-time ministry and believed that going to seminary was my next step of preparation. After all, most positions I was interested in at the time required a seminary degree. So my wife and I left in spring 2005 for Fort Worth, Texas, and I enrolled in Southwestern Baptist Theological Seminary.

Leaving Indiana Avenue Baptist Church was difficult, but I wouldn't realize until later that a connection made there would radically impact my life and eLife's transition into DMM.

One of Indiana Avenue Baptist Church's mission partners while I attended there was an organization I referred to in chapter 4. The leader of this organization would later become one of my mentors who would inspire us to pursue DMM in America. He's been a part of a movement that's seen more than ten million people baptized over the last twenty-five years. My mom had actually served on the board of this organization, and my dad had become friends with the man who had helped catalyze this

He's been a part of a movement that's seen more than ten million people baptized over the last twenty-five years.

great movement of God. This connection would later become vital in bringing eLife into our second decade.

Chapter 22

Seminary Elective

My goal in seminary was to get out as fast as I could. Not that I didn't love attending seminary, I just loved ministry so much more! Because I had been a part of a thriving college ministry, putting all of that on hold for a few years for a seminary degree was tough.

I would max out the number of classes they'd let me take per semester at Southwestern Seminary. Then I'd enroll in Southern Seminary online to take more classes on top of those. A typical semester for me was over twenty hours of classes. The Masters of Divinity is typically a three-year degree, but I plowed through in about two years. As I said, I was eager to get back to ministry, and I thought seminary was a part of what I needed to get back on that track. Although I was able to get through the program quickly, I don't recommend doing it that way, simply because of the sheer amount of information you have to take in.

In my last semester of seminary classes, I needed one more elective. I didn't really care what it was; I just needed to take one more class. I had already taken most of the electives that were offered, and the only one I remember being available was called Church Planting. I thought it was a class on botany—learning to plant flowers at churches—which sounded great.

I enrolled in that class, and I realized it was actually about starting new churches. Where I was from no one really planted churches, at least no one I knew. I mean, there were already tons of churches in my city, so why would anyone go through the effort to start another one?

One of the first books we read in the class was called *Starting Reproducing Congregations*. The book was written by the professor, and I was intrigued by what I read.[1] Later that semester our class attended a church planting conference at nearby Northwood Church.[2]

At the conference, the speakers shared about a concept of church planting I had never heard before. They called these churches *simple churches*. These churches had a simple structure. There were no elaborate buildings or monster budgets. They met in homes, gyms, or businesses—anywhere, really.

The leaders of simple churches were just ordinary people. Extraordinary speaking gifts and a lifetime of pastoral experience were not required to start one. You didn't even have to have a seminary degree. I was shocked because I had been under the impression that a seminary degree was necessary to do anything in ministry. Simple churches were also reproducible. Their simplicity allowed them to multiply quickly.

Listening to the presentation, I was totally in awe. I had never heard of anything like that before. I remember sitting there at that conference and hearing the Lord whisper to me, *I want you to start a church like that.*

I wanted to trust God, but I worried that I could never do that. How would I provide for my family? Where would we meet? What would we do? *Really, Lord? Me?*

The impression on my heart was so strong that I told my wife when I got back to our apartment. I figured she'd think I was crazy. But I was shocked by her response. She said, "I think the Lord is leading us to do that too." What was just supposed to be an elective class was suddenly changing the direction of my life.

I soon began to wonder what to do next. Sure, I had attended the church planting class and learned a lot from the conference, but let's be real. I had no idea how to plant a church. I had no idea where to start.

As I was sitting one day in a seminary chapel service, I saw a brochure with an advertisement on it about a church in Fort Worth that devoted itself to planting churches. The brochure listed a man named Sam Douglass as one of the pastors. I kept that flyer and decided to call him on my way home and ask him if he'd help me figure out how to start a new church.

I remember driving north on Bryant Irvin Road in Fort Worth, across Interstate 20, when Sam answered the phone. I shared with him the story about feeling called to plant a church. With no clue how Sam would respond, I asked if he would help me. He said he'd be glad to.

Sam and I started meeting weekly at a donut shop off McCart Avenue in Fort Worth, and he began to coach me. He asked where I thought I wanted to plant this church, and I told him either Frisco, Texas, or Round Rock, Texas. Then he asked me a question I wasn't expecting.

"Have you considered going back home to Lubbock?"

Going home to Lubbock had never crossed my mind. I'm not really sure why. I just assumed Lubbock had enough churches and didn't need another one. Also, doesn't it say in the Bible that a prophet isn't accepted in his hometown?

Sam encouraged me to do some research on the number of people who go to church in Lubbock and at least pray about it. So that's what I did. I was surprised to find that most people in Lubbock don't go to church, especially people in their twenties. I was in my twenties at the time, and I was really bothered that many people my age weren't interested in following Jesus.

My wife and I decided that we'd drive to Lubbock and spend some time praying about whether the Lord would want us to go back there. After driving around the city, praying, we felt certain the Lord was leading us to come back to my hometown to start a church.

We moved back to Lubbock in March 2007 and started a small group meeting in our home. Soon we outgrew our home and moved into multiple homes. Then we started meeting monthly in a skating rink. Our grand opening was in September of that year, and more than three hundred people came.

> *Somewhere along the way we lost the "simple" vision and became very complex.*

Although the church started pretty simply, and was therefore reproducible, as time went on things began to shift. Somewhere along the way we lost the "simple" vision and became very complex—staff, budgets, buildings, services, crowds, lights, cameras, and soon, campuses.

The explosive growth was exciting, but it wasn't simple. The church had lost its ability to reproduce easily. It seemed there was no turning back.

Chapter 23

From Simple to Complex

S o, you may ask, how did our small church go from simple
to anything but?

As I was preparing to plant a church, I was inspired by
what I read about cell churches around the world. Authors
such as Ralph Neighbour[1] and Joel Comiskey[2] used Scripture
and experience to convince me that "simple" was the way to
go. In part, that's why we started out committed to simplicity.

In fact, contrary to conventional wisdom, we started eLife
with small cell groups rather than big gatherings. We thought
we might have a celebration on occasion to bring the cells
together, but the keyword was *might*. Initially, I wasn't sure if
we'd do celebrations. I envisioned keeping the focus on small,
simple groups or churches that could easily reproduce.

There was only one problem.

As soon as we moved out of houses and into the skating
rink, crowds showed up. Sure, we had sent out some mailers
inviting people to the new church. We had knocked on doors
in several neighborhoods and invited people. We had people
telling their friends. But we were still shocked when more
than three hundred showed up to our grand opening. Then

we were shocked when we grew to more than a thousand in the first year. Imagine our shock when we grew to more than two thousand. Then three thousand and four thousand.

We were listed in *Outreach Magazine* as one of the "100 Fastest-Growing Churches in America" for five of our first ten years. In 2009, just two years after we started, we were the eighth fastest-growing church in the nation overall and the number one fastest-growing church in the nation by percentage gain at 186% growth. In 2010, we were the second fastest-growing church in the nation overall.[3] Our gatherings were exploding and, as a result, "simple" took a backseat to "complex."

How could we ignore all the crowds that were coming? Of course we'd never turn anyone away! We needed big buildings that could hold all of us. We needed a big staff that could minister to all the people. We needed a big budget to fund all of this.

With greater complexity, the church became more difficult to reproduce. It became something that would be difficult for ordinary people to imitate. And it was much more expensive.

> With greater complexity, the church became more difficult to reproduce.

Don't get me wrong— thousands of people heard the gospel in our first ten years. Thousands of people were baptized. Thousands of people heard teaching from God's Word. The Lord used it, no doubt. This was a great thing, but we began to realize that it was not, and likely would not, result in generational disciple making, which is the key to movement and the focus of the Great Commission. Without generational disciple making, we knew there was no way to reach our entire people group.

If we truly wanted to be brave and ask the WIGTake question, this complexity surely wasn't going to be the answer. The answer would be what I sensed the answer was early on. *Simple, reproducible, free, and something ordinary people can do.*

About seven years in, I took our leadership team to Dallas for a retreat. We had planned to spend time together praying and asking God to speak to us about the future of eLife. As we evaluated everything our church did, and with the Great Commission in mind, we talked about what God was doing in India, which we knew about because we had a mission partner there who had reached millions. I remember asking the question, "What would it take for us to see a great movement of God in America like they're seeing in India and other places around the world?" We didn't know the answer to that question, but we knew who would: David Watson. David was one of the initial catalysts for the great movement of God that had spread across India. We needed to bring him in.

When we returned from our retreat, I arranged for David to fly to Lubbock to talk to us about what was happening in India. We spent a day listening to amazing stories about what God is doing there and processing what it would look like to "raise the sails" for something like that to happen here.

We walked away from that meeting convinced that "movements" would likely be the future direction and vision for eLife. We started reading tons of books, articles, and dissertations written by people who have been a part of these international movements. Around that time we connected with Stan, who would later become our DMM coach. And we began to develop the next ten-year vision that we believed would allow us to raise the sails to reach the million.

Some people ask, "Why would you change things if they

have been so successful? Don't you typically change things when they're not working?"

In response, I typically talk about something I'd do at the beginning of each year in our first ten years. I'd usually preach a "vision" message where I'd go over our church's vision again. I'd explain why we started the church, what we were setting out to accomplish, and why we thought our strategy would get us there.

You probably won't be surprised to learn that the Scripture passage used for that message almost every year was the Great Commission in Matthew 28. While pastors might argue all day long about how to accomplish the Great Commission, virtually all of them agree that the Great Commission describes the mission of the church. Churches are supposed to be about making disciples of all the nations. Period. I haven't met a pastor yet who disagrees with that.

As I'd share this passage with our church, I'd often say that the reason we do what we do at eLife is because we've found it's the best way to accomplish what we're supposed to be doing as a church; namely, fulfilling the Great Commission. I told the congregation that every question they had about why we did something a certain way could be answered in this way. We felt that our strategy was the best strategy we knew to accomplish the mission Jesus had given us. But I always put in a caveat. I would be sure to say it's the best strategy we've *found*. And then I would say, "So, if we ever find a strategy that we think will do a better job of helping us accomplish the Great Commission, we'll gladly abandon everything we are doing and switch." I preached that message over and over again.

So why would we change things if they have been so successful (at least in the eyes of American church pastors and

Christians)? *Because we felt we found a better way to accomplish the mission Jesus had given us.*

We heard about millions coming to Christ all over the world and whole communities being transformed by the gospel. Although eLife had reached thousands, proof existed that we could reach many, many more. And what was the key in virtually all of these places? Movements of God. Multiple streams of more than four generations of disciple and church reproduction, leading to thousands or millions of disciples made and thousands or hundreds of thousands of churches being planted.

> *Because we felt we found a better way to accomplish the mission Jesus had given us.*

Obviously God was blessing these movement efforts all over the world. The only problem was that there weren't many documented movements in America. There were tons in Asia. Tons in Africa. Even quite a few in Europe. But hardly any in America. So, why not here, God? Why not now?

That very question began our journey from complex back to simple. We're now asking the WIGTake question, "raising the sails" for movement, and asking God to do in our country what he's doing around the world!

Chapter 24

Identity Crisis

I need to be honest. Transitioning a church to DMM is going to cost you. Big-time. Just as Jesus encouraged the crowd in Luke 14 to count the cost before deciding to become his disciple, you need to count the cost before engaging in DMM. Jesus went so far as to say, "Those of you who do not give up everything you have cannot be my disciples" (Luke 14:33 NIV). DMM essentially invites people not to just call themselves disciples of Jesus but to actually *be* disciples of Jesus. And Jesus said you can't be one of his disciples unless you're willing to give up everything you have.

You must be willing to give up everything you have and everything the church has

> *DMM invites people not to just call themselves disciples of Jesus but to actually be disciples of Jesus.*

if you want to take this journey. Don't take the journey without a lot of prayer, fasting, and soul searching; it's costly. Jesus said it would be. I absolutely believe it's worth it, but it's costly.

In *The Kingdom Unleashed*, David Broodryk, a pastor who embraced DMM, describes the process of pursuing DMM this way:

I really do think that entry into DMM is a death experience: unless the seed falls to the ground and dies, it can bear no fruit. It's a death experience, a complete shift to change to the DMM approach. But the problem is, you can't risk failure without that; risking failure in itself is a sort of death experience. If who you are is dependent on whether this thing works or fails, then you will never take a risk, you'll never do it. But if your identity is in Christ, then you say, "I'm going to try this; if it works, great, He gets the glory; and if it doesn't work—well, it didn't work, but I am still secure in who I am in Him."

Most leaders haven't done that, they are not secure in who they are in Him. Their security is based on the success or failure of what they do. And then that thinking makes you unwilling to take any risks. You also become afraid to give everything away without expecting anything in return. You become trapped by protecting your reputation—but DMM demands all those things. You are no longer building your reputation, you're not building your income, your business, you aren't building fame, not any of those things. You might plant 100,000 churches, but still nobody knows your name.

This is not going to work, it's not going to fly if your identity is in the *ministry*, if your identity is not firmly rooted in *Christ*. But when you root your identity in Him, then you can plant a million churches and no one knows your name and no one cares—and it's not a problem. This is an extremely core issue. It is very significant for us.[1]

Based on my experience so far, describing the transition into DMM as a "death experience" is accurate. The book's author, Jerry Trousdale, describes a resistance that leaders have to overcome in order to embrace DMM. Resistance can come from your denomination, theological traditions, habits, models of ministry, worldview, or anything else that can tend to resist change. It can also come from more personal sources such as friends who resist the vision or even your own church who might not like the new direction.

Jesus said, "Unless a kernel of wheat is planted in the soil and dies, it remains alone. But its death will produce many new kernels—a plentiful harvest of new lives" (John 12:24). While seeing your identity, your ministry, or your church face a "death experience" may seem undesirable, what if by its death a plentiful harvest of new lives is produced? What if God has to take your church down this road to prepare you to plant many new churches? Are you willing to let him take you on that journey?

Before jumping right into DMM, I hope you'll spend plenty of time in prayer and fasting. Again, pursuing DMM is costly, *What if God has to take your church down this road to prepare you to plant many new churches?* and I've experienced that cost firsthand over the last few years.

Additionally, leaders, it's likely that you're going to have an identity crisis if you pursue DMM, much like Broodryk described previously. I experienced it. Our entire staff experienced it.

You may feel as if DMM goes against everything you were

taught in seminary. As if it goes against everything you experienced in churches growing up. As if it goes against everything you thought was right, sacred, and the way things must be done. It challenges most of your assumptions.

As a result, if your identity is tied up in what you were taught in seminary, what you experienced in church growing up, or how you think things have to be done, everything you "know" to be true will be turned on its head.

Remember, however, that most of us get our identity tied up in in the wrong things. Our identity should be fully rooted in Jesus Christ, rather than in what we do, how much we make, or what people think of us. If your identity is rooted in anything other than Jesus, you're in a dangerous place. Let me give you an example of how this looked for someone on our team.

If your identity is rooted in anything other than Jesus, you're in a dangerous place.

Tamara was raised in church. She loved the church and loved ministry so much that she moved to California to pursue a master's degree from a seminary in the Bay Area. She had a passion for children's ministry and was excited when we offered her the opportunity to become the Children's Minister at our Downtown Campus.

Tamara knew a lot about children's ministry. She had been a part of one as a child. She had studied more about children's ministry in seminary. And we were hiring her to lead ours. She was confident in what she was doing and felt that she knew the best way to minister to children. Not only that, she felt she knew the best way to "do" church. Obviously, conventional wisdom told Tamara that the best way to "do" church is like what you experienced growing up, what you were taught in seminary, or what everyone else is doing.

Without realizing it, Tamara had gotten her identity tied up in how to do children's ministry and even how to do church. It's who she was. It's who she had spent her life wanting to become.

When I first cast vision to our staff for DMM, without knowing it, I launched Tamara into an identity crisis. I'm sure it felt that the foundation on which she had built her life, namely, the American church model of ministry, had just been pulled out from under her. Her mind began to swirl. If the American church is failing to accomplish its mission, is she a failure? Was her seminary degree a waste? Has she been a part of the problem? Was she actually wrong about the *best* way to do church? To critique the American church was to critique her. Acknowledging that the American church has failed in many ways was acknowledging that *she* has failed.

Tamara had to go through a season of unraveling her identity from a model of ministry. She knew her identity was ultimately in Christ, but this new vision exposed that she had falsely placed her identity in things she never should have. But, we reminded Tamara, she wasn't the only one. All of us had. We had fallen in love with a way of doing things, and we didn't realize that we associated ourselves so closely with that way of doing things that to challenge the method was to challenge *us*. This was a big problem.

Around that same time, Tamara was invited to participate in one of our Phase One Goer Groups. One of the practices of these groups is "going out among the lost." She did that with her group and met some internationals with whom she was able to share. She had the opportunity to read the Bible with people who had never read it before. It was such a powerful and eye-opening experience for Tamara that it caused her heart to open to DMM. God began to grip her with the reality that unless we see a Disciple Making Movement, people in her own country and people in other countries may never follow Jesus. She became convinced that DMM was the key!

Through the process, she was able to root her identity back in Christ alone and has become one of the most vocal proponents of the DMM vision. Her passion for DMM, though, began with an identity crisis.

Leaders, a cost is involved in pursuing DMM, not only for you, but for your entire team. When some of your people experience the identity crisis, they may leave you. They may feel that because you have chosen a "new way" of doing ministry, you're attacking the old way, and as a result you're attacking them, since their identity is tied up in the old way. That's a cost you'll have to count.

After having led many staff members unintentionally through an identity crisis over the past couple of years, many of us are now at a point where we believe it was totally worth it. Not only that, we're thankful for it. We are glad it led us through a season of making sure our identity isn't wrapped up in *any* model of ministry. This process was a necessary part of our team's preparing to embrace DMM in our next ten years.

In the next couple of chapters I will tell about some of the other costs we experienced and why we continued to believe the vision was worth it, regardless of the cost.

Buckle your seatbelt!

Chapter 25

A Reduction in Giving

Pursuing DMM will cost you financially. It's almost a guarantee.

As we began shifting to the DMM strategy, I was so thankful for how financially conservative eLife has been over the years, giving us the margin to follow the Lord however he would lead. For years, we've operated with a significant amount of money in reserve. Also, our expenses usually come in far below our income each year. We never had much debt as a church; and any of the debt we did have, we were able to pay off in just a few years.

Choosing to be fiscally conservative positioned our church to be able to make this change. I've talked to other pastors interested in what we're doing, and when they learned there would be a financial cost, they reluctantly had to back away. Many churches have loads of debt, are consistently over budget, and are not fiscally conservative enough to be able to weather a big financial loss.

A word to pastors and leaders: I'd strongly encourage you to lead your church to be financially conservative so that you can always follow the Lord wherever he leads, even if that results in financial loss. If your church is strapped with loads of debt and other financial obligations, it may miss out on something new the Lord is doing simply because it is enslaved to the current model of ministry.

Years ago, as we were making conservative financial decisions, I had no idea eLife would be at this point. I just knew we needed to save and spend in such a way that we were always prepared to follow the Lord wherever he led. I didn't want to be a slave to debt, and I don't want you to be one either. Imagine what the Lord might invite you and your church to be a part of if you make the financial room to join him.

Our staff usually begins working on the budget in the fall before the year kicks off. Typically, before we start the process, our Executive Pastor, who is also a CPA, will come up with an amount of projected contributions for the upcoming year. To make his projections, he assesses our current giving trends and anything coming up in the future that may affect those trends.

By budget time in the fall of 2016, we knew that 2017 would be the year that we would lead our church to go "all in" with movements. We knew this transition would cost us financially. Not because movements are expensive but because we were planning to train and send out fifty-four DMM Church Planters and their teams as a part of our ten-year anniversary service in September of 2017.

You see, the fifty-four church planters would be some of our church's most generous givers. And they would be leaving our church and taking their giving with them. Not only would they leave, but we were encouraging each individual to recruit a team to go too. That meant we could be intentionally sending up to five hundred of our attendees and givers out into the field. That's a ton of money that would be walking out of our church.

While it would've been impossible to project to what extent contributions would be reduced if we sent that many people out, John did some calculations, and he came up with a reasonable estimate. We then took his projected giving for 2017 and subtracted all of the money we expected to leave the church in that year. That way we were prepared for people to be sent out and take their giving with them and were able to adjust our spending accordingly.

In addition to sending out many individuals who would no longer give to our church, we also anticipated that when we cast the vision at our ten-year anniversary, many people wouldn't want to take this next journey with us. And we totally understood and supported that. However, people transitioning to other great churches in the area would also result in a reduction in giving.

In the end, 2017 was an amazing year, and we were so glad that in our preparation we had made budget adjustments. As a result, we weren't scrambling when people started to leave. We were able to joyfully send out many church planters. We were also able to bless many people as they told us they were going to move on to another church.

As we move forward, we always want to make sure there is enough margin in our budget to continue to send out church planting teams. We never want to encourage someone to stay with us just because we can't afford to lose their giving. We want to live so far below our means that when *anyone* says he or she feels God's leading to join a church planting team, we gladly encourage that person to go for it.

Honestly, I never thought I'd lead a church where we'd be celebrating people leaving even more than we celebrate people coming. But, in truth, sending people out on a disciple-making mission is far more exciting than seeing people sit comfortably in a chair each weekend, far from the people who need Jesus the most.

Honestly, I never thought I'd lead a church where we'd be celebrating people leaving even more than we celebrate people coming.

Although the transition to DMM isn't easy, and the costs are high, the transition is worth it.

Chapter 26

A Reduction in Attendance

C hances are, if you lead an American church, DMM is
going to move things in the opposite direction of how
you've led the church to this point. A focus on disciple making is going to make an impact in every area of your church. I
think it will be a positive impact, and so do many others. But
you'll find that many will also disagree.

Anytime something changes, some people are going to be
unhappy. That's not necessarily a bad thing. Different people have different opinions and varying tolerance levels for
change. Some people love change. They're the early adopters.
Anytime change is announced, they're the first to jump on
board. Other people despise change. No matter how well you
do at casting vision, these people are not going to catch the
vision, and they're going to do their best to undermine it. And
there will be people at all points in between.

As you know, we led our American church in one way
for the first ten years and then announced at the ten-year
anniversary that our Leadership Team felt God was giving
us a different vision for the next ten years. However, this
announcement wasn't as sudden as it sounds. As I mentioned

in previous chapters, we had slowly dripped the vision to our church through the year leading up to that service in various sermon series. The ten-year anniversary was just the event where we made the formal announcement of the vision change.

We knew that some people who had signed on for the vision for the first ten years wouldn't be interested in pursuing the vision for the second ten and would choose to move on. We knew that others would be so excited for this new vision and the opportunity to reach even more people that they would want to get started right away.

The American church has "done" church the same way for so long that any kind of major change is going to be tough. When you start changing what people grew up with, what they've done their whole lives, and what has felt like a constant, people feel uncomfortable. If their lives were positively impacted doing church a certain way, it's only natural to think they would prefer to keep it that way.

Also, you may be surprised to learn that some people tend to think that their preferred way of doing church is the "biblical" way. That gets dangerous, because once someone believes they have found the "biblical," a.k.a. "right," way of doing anything, there's very little chance they will be open to change.

Yet, in reality, if you read through the New Testament with a fresh lens and without a certain type of church in mind, I can almost guarantee you won't immediately think of the way Americans do church. Buildings. Budgets. Staff. These things are not in there. That doesn't mean the way we do church is wrong. God has blessed a lot of different types of churches throughout church history. It just means that claiming that you've found the "biblical" way by following the American model is a little shortsighted. Again, this makes it likely that you'd never be open to a better strategy for fulfilling the Great Commission if one was to come along.

Because of all this, we tried to approach the implementation of the vision as slowly as we could. The overall vision-casting process took several years before we even made the announcement. Then, after making the announcement,

If you read through the New Testament with a fresh lens and without a certain type of church in mind, I can almost guarantee you won't immediately think of the way Americans do church.

we spent a year making gradual changes to bring people along slowly. But, despite this, many decided this wasn't for them and they moved on. At that point the issue becomes about how you handle folks walking away.

Sometimes attendees expect that if you tell your pastor or the church staff that you're moving on, you'll be met with questions like, "Wait a minute. What can we do to keep you? Is there something we can change? Is there something we can do to keep you happy?" We didn't take this approach. We believed that if God spoke to people and encouraged them to leave, we'd bless them, support them, pray for them, tell them we understood, and send them off to the next assignment God had for them.

Our church is much larger than the average church, so we knew our reduction in attendance could be much greater. We ended up having thousands of people walk out the doors in the year following the announcement of the new vision. Some were the people we trained in DMM who were being sent to join DMM church planting teams, and others were leaving to attend a different church. But, regardless of your church's size, there will be an attendance reduction if you choose to pursue DMM. Not everyone is going to catch the vision. And that's okay! Remember, in this case, a small number of people catching the vision is plenty because movements are built on multiplication.

You may find that some people who did not catch the vision initially and chose to leave will catch it eventually and come back with a desire to join you. When I first started eLife, people thought I was insane. They thought our attractional model of ministry was crazy. I'm sure many people thought, *There's no way that's going to work.* But, a few years later, as God used our church to reach many for Christ, I think some of those same people became less skeptical and began to cheer us on.

Isn't that how it works with any new idea? Initially the new idea is met with skepticism and criticism; and then over time, if the idea becomes successful, it's met with admiration and emulation. The key is perseverance!

While a reduction in attendance can be painful to watch and experience, here's the good news: God is pruning you. The purpose of pruning, even though it can be painful, is so that you can bear more fruit.

> *The purpose of pruning, even though it can be painful, is so that you can bear more fruit.*

Think about Jesus. He spoke to crowds much larger than most American pastors are probably speaking to. But when things got tough or when Jesus called for a higher level of commitment, the crowds all went running. Guess how many Jesus had at the end? About 120 gathered in an upper room in Acts 1.

Was Jesus a failure? Of course not! Then why didn't he

still have large crowds following him in Acts 1? Because he told the crowds some things that likely scared them to death. As an example, he said that if they wanted to follow him and be his disciples, they'd have to give up everything they had (Luke 14:33). That message will empty out a building in a hurry! Not everyone wanted to give up everything they had. Not everyone was willing to put aside their traditions and preferences.

If the key to a movement was keeping the crowds happy, Jesus wouldn't have said some of the things he said. He wouldn't have told people to deny themselves, take up their cross, and follow him (Matthew 16:24 NIV). And he certainly wouldn't have told them to eat his flesh and drink his blood (John 6:53–58). In fact, John said, "At this point many of his disciples turned away and deserted him" (verse 66).

Typically, in the American church, we don't consider a leader to be "successful" if people turn away and desert the leader—but this was part of Jesus' strategy. He was going to speak the *"Focus on a few to win many."* truth and see who really wanted to give up everything and follow him. He would hand those people the Great Commission, and our world hasn't been the same since. It doesn't take everyone catching the vision. In fact, one often-repeated DMM principle is, "Focus on a few to win many."

Jerry Trousdale, in *Miraculous Movements*, describes it this way:

> Westerners are in love with well-packaged mass
> marketing of the gospel. In church, as in adver-
> tising, growth is a numbers game about getting

159

as many impressions as possible out to the masses. Mass communication and evangelism may have their place, but they show no signs of dramatically transforming the world. But Jesus gave almost all of His attention to intentionally discipling just twelve men, especially focusing on four of them. The results speak for themselves. Can we do better, investing in Christian mass messaging and once-a-week preaching services?[1]

Crowds are fickle. Jesus' ministry proved that. One day they're admiring you, and the next day they're calling for your crucifixion. That's why Jesus spent most of his time with his disciples. He knew that eleven of these men, not the crowds, were the key to reaching the world. Jesus spent a vast majority of his time (as detailed in the Gospels) with the disciples, away from the crowds. He knew the key to getting the good news out into all the world was to focus on the most serious and committed people, those who were willing to give up everything they had and follow him.

Change is hard, but if God is leading, it's always worth it.

Recently, as I was scrolling through my Twitter feed, I came across a quote from a Christian author that is fitting here. He tweeted, "Pastors, you will always discover a church's idols by changing things. People may leave. Programs may stop. Giving may drop. Gossips may divide. Activists may undermine. Staff may revolt. You be courageous."[2]

Change is hard, but if God is leading, it's always worth it.

Are you willing to be courageous? Are you willing to count the cost? Are you willing to give up everything you have, including your church's atten-dance count, to Jesus? Are you willing to watch half your church leave, if that's what it takes for you to pursue this disciple-making vision? When you call people to give up everything they have, the crowds will often desert you. The disciple makers are the ones who will stick with you. And the disciple makers are the ones who are needed to see a movement of God in your city.

Are you willing to watch half your church leave, if that's what it takes for you to pursue this disciple-making vision?

Chapter 27

Doubts and Discouragement

If you journey into DMM, you will definitely face doubts and discouragement along the way. The doubts can sound like this, especially as you're dealing with the costs I mentioned in the previous chapters.

> *Is this really worth it?*
> *Am I sure I heard the Lord correctly?*
> *What if this doesn't work?*
> *Am I setting myself up to fail?*
> *Are people even interested in disciple making?*
> *What if everyone abandons me?*
> *Can this even happen in America?*

Doubts aren't fun. But I've found that my doubts drive me to the Lord for reaffirmation of the vision. And that's a good place to be.

Over the past few years that we've been pursuing DMM, I've had my fair share of doubts. Some of them sounded like the ones mentioned previously. Each time they have brought me to my knees with a desperate request for God to reaffirm what he's told our team and me to do. And guess what has happened almost every time? Through Scripture, prayer, other believers, mentors, or disciple-making books, God has reaffirmed the vision. My doubt dissipates, and I get back to doing what I originally felt God had told us to do.

The Lord has given our team so much reaffirmation over the last few years that I remember praying recently, *Lord, we're going through a tough time right now, but you don't even have to give more affirmation if you don't want. You've given us so much already. We'll keep persevering even when it gets hard! Seeing our people group reached is worth any cost!*

I'm encouraged by Matthew 28:16–17, which says, "Then the eleven disciples left for Galilee, going to the mountain where Jesus had told them to go. When they saw him, they worshiped him—but some of them doubted!" The disciples witnessed Jesus' life, his teaching, his miracles, his death, and his resurrection, and some of them still doubted. Isn't that crazy?

Do you know the good news? In the next three verses, he still gives this group of doubting disciples the Great Commission. This makes me glad that doubts don't disqualify us.

Just remember, as you pursue DMM you will have doubts. Let those doubts draw you to Jesus rather than away from your mission.

Not only will you struggle with doubt on your journey toward movement, you're also very likely to face discouragement. I've found the greatest discouragement comes when people whom you love and whom you've done ministry with for years decide to move on. People in your church. People on your staff. People in your family. Good friends, both on our staff and in our church, have decided to leave. That's totally okay. Don't let that discourage you. It's going to happen . . . a lot. God can lead you and that person in two different directions.

Here's the truth. Just because God has given *you* a particular vision doesn't mean he's giving everyone else that same vision. He can lead people to pursue different visions. And that's okay. As mentioned in the previous chapter, what matters is what you do with the news that people are moving on—and that still holds true when they are close to you or have been with you for a long time. Remember, it's not that they're wrong and you're right. You can both be right. Bless them. Encourage them. Support them. Send them. You want them to pursue the vision God has given them, even if it's not the vision God has given you.

Having said that, don't let conversations with those who are choosing to leave overshadow all the people in the church who are excited about the new vision. Sometimes we only hear from the people who aren't on board with the vision and not the people who are fired up to chase the vision with us. Don't let the voices of those who leave overshadow all the voices of people who stay.

Also, remember this. A pastor's most important job is to lead the church's elders or Leadership Team to seek the Lord, listen to his voice,

> *Don't let the voices of those who leave overshadow all the voices of people who stay.*

do what he says, and leave the consequences up to him. You aren't the Senior Pastor. Jesus is! He gets to decide the direction of his church, and the job of the leadership is to listen and obey.

What all Christians *should* want most from their pastors and leaders is that they're seeking the Lord, hearing from him, and casting *his* vision to *his* church. Notice I said what all Christians *should* want. If we're being honest, what all Christians *should* want is not what all Christians actually *do* want. Many Christians want the leaders of their church to do what *they* want them to do. They want to attend a church that *they* like. They want to attend a church that caters to *their* needs.

> *What all Christians should want most from their pastors and leaders is that they're seeking the Lord, hearing from him, and casting his vision to his church.*

I don't blame the sheep, though, for this attitude. I blame the shepherds. We're the ones who set it up this way. We're the ones who perpetuated this way of doing church. The American church is widely criticized for being consumeristic. And there's a lot of truth in this.

The traditional American church model is not primarily "missionary" in nature, where the goal is to "produce" rather than to "consume." If you look at the way 99 percent of worship centers are built in our country, you'll see rows of chairs facing a platform at the front where people stand to perform and give the people sitting in those rows something good to "consume." When the performance is not as good as it used to be, the consumers move on. Many American pastors I know would admit how consumeristic our church system is, but most are at a loss as to how to change it.

> *Many American pastors I know would admit how consumeristic our church system is, but most are at a loss as to how to change it.*

When pastors or elders initiate change at a church, most people are thinking about whether *they* like it, not whether the pastors or elders have heard from the Lord. That's very dangerous, but it's often true. We need to shepherd people away from this. It's Jesus' church, not ours. We need to do what he wants, not what we want. It's not about us. It's about him. We need the pastors and elders who are leading Jesus' church to be free to listen to Jesus and do what he says whether everybody likes it or not. As pastors, we must obey the Lord and leave the consequences up to him. It's his church, not ours.

Jerry Trousdale warns us of the opposition that can come when we follow the Lord into a disciple-making vision:

> Experience shows that the opposition to Disciple Making Movements often comes not only from the outside but from Christians who do not understand it or who reject its premises. DMM practitioners have been ostracized from their denominations, have lost friends, have been vilified and slandered, all from within the Christian community.
>
> As Christians grow in their discipleship, opposition from both inside and outside the church is inevitable, and we need to be ready for it.[1]

Are you ready for it? Have you counted the cost?

Remember these encouraging words: "This is my command—be strong and courageous! Do not be afraid or discouraged. For the LORD your God is with you wherever you go" (Joshua 1:9).

Chapter 28

PIPSY

After casting vision for DMM and training people, what's next? You send them out among the lost to places where Jesus has led them to go. But what do they do when they get there?

You have to gain access first. The word *access* is used a lot in DMM circles and refers to a reason for being there. When you go to a new place where you don't naturally belong, you need to find some means of access so the people in that place receive you and don't reject you immediately.

Picture this: Jesus has led you to go make disciples in a part of your town where you don't typically go. In fact, if you were to go there, you'd feel very out of place. And the people there would wonder why you're there. You look different. You come from a different background. You have different cultural norms. Maybe you don't even speak the language that is spoken predominantly. If you go into that part of town, you need a reason to be there. You need *access* so that the people in that part of town don't reject you as soon as you arrive. So that your reason for being there causes people not to be so skeptical of your presence.

The goal of gaining access is to find persons of peace, who start groups with their oikos, which become churches that multiply generationally.

The goal of gaining access is to find persons of peace.

Remember, Stan is the one who said, "Around the world, the number one way DMMers find those interested in God is by serving them (healing prayer, kind deed, community service) while consistently, simultaneously, and culturally appropriately pointing to God." Stan trained us to gain access by serving people through praying for healing for the sick and/or meeting practical needs in the area. This comes straight from the "Jesus strategy" in Matthew 10 and Luke 10: "If you enter a town and it welcomes you, eat whatever is set before you. Heal the sick, and tell them, 'The Kingdom of God is near you now'" (Luke 10:8–9).

The primary way Jesus taught his disciples to gain access in new areas is by healing the sick. You can imagine that if you enter a place where you don't belong and heal their sick, they will likely receive you immediately as a friend. You've served them in an extraordinary way, and they're eternally grateful. As the disciples would heal the sick, people's hearts would be open to the message about the kingdom of God.

As we enter new places, we are training people to do what Jesus said to do—heal the sick or meet some practical need and then proclaim the kingdom of God. We do both, not either/or. Stan pointed out that some people enter new places and just serve people without proclaiming the Kingdom, while other people enter new places and just proclaim the Kingdom without serving people. He said, "You don't want to work with one hand tied behind your back. Do both!"

How do you decide where to go? Look at Luke 10:1: "The Lord now chose seventy-two other disciples and sent them ahead in pairs to all the towns and places he planned to visit." We go to the places Jesus has prepared for us to go, just as the disciples went to the places Jesus planned to visit. We pray and listen to Jesus for direction.

As we enter new places, we are training people to do what Jesus said to do—heal the sick or meet some practical need and then proclaim the kingdom of God.

We want to join him where he's already working, and we trust that he will lead us to those places.

One thing we've realized is that Jesus has already revealed in Scripture the types of places where he's already likely to be working. In fact, he tells us when we visit these places and help these people it's as if we're actually helping him.

Do you remember what Jesus said about this in Matthew 25?

> But when the Son of Man comes in his glory, and all the angels with him, then he will sit upon his glorious throne. All the nations will be gathered in his presence, and he will separate the people as a shepherd separates the sheep from the goats. He will place the sheep at his right hand and the goats at his left.
>
> Then the King will say to those on his right, "Come, you who are blessed by my Father, inherit the Kingdom prepared for you from the creation of the world. For I was hungry, and you fed me. I was thirsty, and you gave me a drink. I was a stranger, and you invited me into your home. I

was naked, and you gave me clothing. I was sick, and you cared for me. I was in prison, and you visited me."

Then these righteous ones will reply, "Lord, when did we ever see you hungry and feed you? Or thirsty and give you something to drink? Or a stranger and show you hospitality? Or naked and give you clothing? When did we ever see you sick or in prison and visit you?"

And the King will say, "I tell you the truth, when you did it to one of the least of these my brothers and sisters, you were doing it to me!" (Matthew 25:31–40)

Jesus said that to serve these people is to serve him. To go to these people is to go to him. And in movements, we want to be where *he* is!

Our DMM teams like to remember these groups of people Jesus described by using the acronym PIPSY.

The first *P* stands for "poor": the hungry, the thirsty, the naked. Jesus said when we feed them, give them something to drink, and clothe them, it's as if we're doing it to him. It rings true to us that Jesus is often working among the poor because one of my DMM coaches shared that virtually every known movement in the world has started among the poor. God cares about the poor, and part of the mission of the Messiah who was prophesied in the Old Testament is that he would proclaim the good news to the poor. Note in Isaiah 61:1:

> The Spirit of the Sovereign LORD is upon me,
>   for the LORD has anointed me

to bring good news to the poor.
He has sent me to comfort the brokenhearted
and to proclaim that captives will be released
and prisoners will be freed.

As we think about places where we want to go and gain access, we start with some of the poorest places in our town, because we know when we go to them, we're going to Jesus (according to Matthew 25). Jesus is working among the poor. Will you join him?

The *I* stands for "international." Internationals are some of the "strangers" among us. They're not from here. They've moved here from other places in the world, and they don't know many people. We've found that they are longing to be invited into an American home. Our church has seen so much fruit when we've invited internationals from the local university into our homes. Or exchange students from around the world. Internationals are often so receptive because they have a need. They're in an unfamiliar place, and they're looking for someone to befriend them. When we invite them into our homes, Jesus says we're essentially inviting him in! He is working among internationals. Will you join him?

The second *P* stands for "prisoner." Jesus said that when we visit the prisoner, we're visiting him. He's already at work among the prisoners. As you might imagine, prisoners are often at a low point in life and can have a deep hunger for spiritual things. In our first ten years, our church started ten campuses, and three of them were in jails. If you were to ask any of our staff which of our campuses seem to consistently have the most remarkable stories, almost everyone would tell you it's our Freedom Campuses (which is what we call our campuses in the jails). Many of our visits to the prison have resulted in men and women being set on fire for God and mobilized to be disciple makers in their neighborhoods when they get out. Jesus is working in the prisons. Will you join him?

The S stands for "sick." According to Matthew 25, when we care for the sick, we're caring for Jesus. As mentioned previously, Jesus' main strategy in Matthew 10 and Luke 10 for his disciples to gain access was healing the sick. When we're looking for places where Jesus is already working, we should look for places with sick people. He's already told us when we go to those places we're going to places where he's moving. Jesus is working among sick people. Will you join him?

The Y doesn't stand for anything—it just turns PIPS into an adjective so we can use it in a sentence. We often talk about a neighborhood being PIPSY or trying to find PIPSY people.

To be clear, individuals do not have to meet every one of these qualifications to be considered PIPSY. They can be poor, international, a prisoner, sick, or a combination of the four to qualify as PIPSY.

Our teams have borne the most fruit going to PIPSY places to gain access. There is no question about it. We didn't start out this way, however. Initially, everyone was going out among the lost, determining the location somewhat arbitrarily. We weren't being intentional about asking the Lord to show us where he had prepared for us to go. We'd just go to a grocery store, a park, or any number of other places and start talking to people. That's not all bad, but we've gotten a lot more strategic lately in the places we've chosen to go.

One thing we consistently found when we became more strategic is that the non-PIPSY places were the least receptive to us. The richer parts of town usually didn't have time for a spiritual conversation with us, and when we asked people if we could pray for them, they often weren't interested. Jesus told us rich people are at a spiritual disadvantage (Matthew 19:23–24). That doesn't mean we should ignore them, but it definitely means that PIPSY areas are likely to bear more fruit. When we started focusing our "going out among the lost" efforts on PIPSY places, we found a greater openness to spiritual conversations, serving people, praying for people, and starting groups.

In the next few chapters, I'll share some incredible stories about some of the PIPSY places our teams have gone.

PIPSY areas are likely to bear more fruit.

Chapter 29

Poor

"Virtually every Church Planting Movement in the world today started among the poor." This statement by Roy, one of my DMM coaches, has always stuck with me. It makes sense, then, that if we want to see movement break out in our country, we should also look for it to happen among the poor.

John, eLife's Executive Pastor, and I are the ones who coach our church's DMM church planting teams. We started recommending to our teams that they begin "going out among the lost" in places where they're likely to find poor people.

> "Virtually every Church Planting Movement in the world today started among the poor." —Roy Moran

Much like Andrew and Kristin, whose story is detailed in chapter 20, several of our teams started going to a Walmart in a poorer part of town to pray for people. As the teams were shopping, they'd ask God to lead them to people to pray for. When they saw someone they wanted to pray for, they'd say, "Hi, my name is _____. We're praying for people as we're shopping for groceries and wanted to see if there's any specific way we can pray for you?" Other times they'd say, "Hi, my name is _____. If God could do a miracle in your life, what would you have him do?" And once they responded, they would say, "Can I pray that he'd do that in your life?" Our teams would often find that people would be receptive to these questions. The person would give our teams some things to pray for. Then the teams would pray for the person in Jesus' name.

If God could do a miracle in your life, what would you have him do?

In our coaching meeting each week, the teams often reported that the people they prayed for would begin to cry. In fact, one team told me that in 90 percent of the cases in which they pray for someone, that person would cry. We talked about how those people were likely being touched by God. It's not every day someone comes up to you and talks to God on your behalf. When that happens, especially if someone has drifted from God, or doesn't know him personally, you can understand how that would be very powerful.

We've found that going out and offering to pray for people is a great way to gauge interest in (and openness to) spiritual things. It identifies us immediately as spiritual people, which Stan told me should happen within the first few minutes of any conversation. Most people, especially if they're PIPSY, are open to prayer. They realize they have needs, and many of them believe God could meet those needs. We've found that after praying for people and comforting them as they cry, they are open to talking about possibly starting a DG with their family and friends.

Since we are looking for "persons of peace," or WOOLY persons, allowing us to pray for them gives us some indication that they are *W* or welcoming. The next thing we want to do is see if they are *OO*, or willing to open their oikos. We then ask the DG question, "Would you be interested in gathering your family and friends together to discover more about God through reading his Word?" Many of our teams will ask the DG question immediately after praying for people. They'll exchange phone numbers and follow up at a later time.

I asked Stan if asking the DG question immediately after praying for someone you just met was asking too soon. He responded, "In movements across the world, the people who get the most groups started are the people who do the most asking. Encourage them to keep asking!"

While talking to people in grocery stores is definitely a way to search for PoPs (persons of peace), we continued to ask the Lord to give us even more strategic avenues of getting to know people. Around that time we saw that Beyond, a missions-sending organization, put out a series of videos delving into the CPM steps. I'd highly recommend you watch these.[1]

> *"The people who get the most groups started are the people who do the most asking."* –Stan Parks

Step 1 is to pray and ask the Lord where he'd have you to go and Step 2 is to begin prayer walking that area. We were convicted that we weren't prayer walking enough. This is an important practice in movements around the world to pre pare the soil for the gospel to be planted.

In addition to going to Walmart or other places where you can find lots of spiritually hungry people, we encouraged our teams to begin to pray and ask God if there was a specific area or neighborhood that he'd have them go (Step 1). Whereas in Walmart you don't usually see the same people again and again, if you continue to go back to the same area or neighborhood, you might find it easier to build relationships. Several of our teams felt that God had placed on their hearts a PIPSY area to focus on, so we encouraged them to begin prayer walking those areas and looking for people to talk to (Step 2). This proved to be fruitful as well.

Our teams would walk up and down streets in these neighborhoods and pray. When they saw someone they could talk to, they would often approach that person and ask the same questions they'd ask people in Walmart. They were looking for opportunities to pray for people.

My team felt God leading us to go to an area that a Lubbock police officer identified as one of the top three most dangerous areas in town. We knew it was a poor area, and we had a real sense that God was preparing people of peace for us there. The first thing we began to do was prayer walk the neighborhood. We'd go out on Thursday afternoons for a few hours and pray. As we saw people around, we'd begin to talk to them and ask if we could pray for them. While we had the opportunity to pray for quite a few people, we found that many people weren't out in the afternoons. We figured they were probably working or staying inside to avoid the heat. We continued to prayer walk, but as we did, we kept asking the Lord for even more strategic opportunities to engage with people.

One day we were driving around praying, and I drove past the middle school in that neighborhood. Then the Lord reminded me of something I had forgotten. We knew one of the people who worked at that school. She was a close friend of ours and the wife of one of our staff members. I figured we could call her and see if she could connect us with some of the families in that neighborhood who had needs.

I talked to her on the phone and asked if there was any way

she could connect us with families in the school to serve. She said that because her school's population is very low income, they have a paid social worker on-site who works with each of the families. She connected me with her immediately.

I called the social worker and told her we were looking for families in the neighborhood whom we could serve. She was excited about our desire to help and said she had many children at the school whose families were deeply in need. She asked me, "How many families do you want?" She was willing to give us as many as we wanted to serve. I could hardly believe it.

I told her we'd like to start with five. Then I told her that we'd like to meet each family in their home, listen to their story, and see how we could help. She told us that she was going to contact five families that she thought would be very interested in having us visit them and then provide their phone numbers to us if they gave permission. All five families she contacted were eager for us to come and see them. They were PIPSY, after all.

We visited each family in their home, listened to their stories, asked them what their needs were, and then we prayed for them. Our team would get together and brainstorm how we could best serve them, and then we'd start meeting needs. We bought groceries, helped with utility bills and rent, assisted them in finding other places to stay, helped them to find jobs, and so on.

As we met each family's needs, we tried to gauge their spiritual interest. We knew their greatest need was a relationship with Jesus, and we tried to be discerning as to who was open to that. Several of them told us they had drifted from Jesus and wanted help getting back on the right track. Others told us they wanted to get back into church again. Some mentioned their desire to be a spiritual leader for their children. For those who were spiritually interested, we would offer to train them to lead a Discovery Group with their family and friends.

We found that connecting with the school and getting into the homes of needy families in the school was by far the most fruitful means we had found for seeing groups start. Because the person at the school was able to make introductions for us, families were eager to have us into their homes and get to know us. They knew we had come in peace and that we wanted to care for and bless their families.

Once we finished with the first five families, we asked for more, and she eagerly gave us more. It seemed as if reports were getting back to the school that we really were helping these families and that we had been a blessing to them (perhaps both physical and spiritually).

We never pressured anyone to do a Discovery Group. We were there to simply serve people and see who was interested. If they were interested, then great. If they weren't, that was okay too. The goal was to serve and meet needs, and we were able to do that for everyone we met.

Other DMM teams heard about our success in going through the schools, so they pursued the schools in their particular neighborhood of focus. They found that virtually every school was eager to have help meeting the needs of struggling families whose children attended. This became our most strategic means of gaining access into these neighborhoods, and we've seen several groups started this way.

Although working through schools has been great, there's another way we've gained access successfully into some of these PIPSY neighborhoods: knocking on doors. While we weren't sure this would be the most strategic means of gaining access, it was more strategic than doing nothing. Plus, the schools were closed for the summer, so we needed a new point of entry.

My team would be the first to tell you that when I shared this idea with them they didn't love it. We were in a rough area, and there was no telling what you'd find behind each door you knocked on. They all agreed to go with me, probably because they didn't feel they had a choice (although they did, I promise!). But several of them admitted afterward that they weren't too excited about it. One of my team members said he tried to find a way to get out of it. He thought about calling in sick or scheduling an appointment or anything to get out of knocking on doors.

Thankfully, my whole team showed up that first day. We huddled to pray before going out, and one of the guys asked, "Are you sure this is a good idea?" I told him I wasn't sure if it was a good idea, but I didn't know any other way to get to talk to more people in the area.

I told them I thought we should start with a certain apartment complex. It had the reputation of being one of the worst in the area. In fact, several people told me that it was where they used to buy drugs before they started following Jesus. They said, "You can get any drug in town in that place." I thought it seemed like the perfect place to start!

My team is a team of four. There were thirty-two apartments. We split up into twos, so each pair took sixteen apartments. We knocked on the door and let people know that we were praying in the area; then we asked if there was any specific thing we could pray about for them or their family.

The response was unbelievable.

The four of us came back together two hours later with more stories and potential opportunities to follow up than we knew what to do with. We all admitted jokingly that we were scared to death, but God had gone before us and created many divine appointments for us.

While we weren't sure if this method of gaining access would be as effective as the contacts we had gotten from the school, it gave us the opportunity to talk to a large number of people, and so we knew we'd keep going back each week. Our strategy in these apartments was the "Jesus strategy" from Luke 10. We wanted to keep going back weekly until one of two things happened: either (1) we found the person of peace, saw a group started, and coached them through starting other groups in the complex so, in time, the whole complex would be reached; or (2) we found little openness and would need to wipe the dust off of our feet (Luke 10:10–11) and move on.

We weren't going to stay there forever. Just long enough to find the person God had prepared and turn the ministry over to them or to find that there was no person of peace there.

We've seen some amazing things happen there so far. Here are just a few of the stories.

The first day we went to the apartment complex, anxieties were high. After we prayed together, before beginning to knock on doors, something happened that affirmed immediately we were supposed to be there. Carol pulled up.

I recognized Carol immediately. She had stopped me at a gas station about a year ago and told me she had seen me on TV and asked me to pray for her. I prayed for her right there and didn't figure I'd ever see her again. In fact, I didn't see her again until she pulled into the apartment complex that day.

She rolled down her window, and I walked up to the car and said hello to her. Surprised, I asked her, "Do you live here?" She said she'd lived there for more than ten years. I told her what we were doing there, and I told her our plan. She said our presence was definitely needed in that apartment complex and that there was a lot of crime taking place there. She started telling us more about it and was able to point out the notoriously dangerous apartments. I told her that I thought God had our paths cross again for a reason and that perhaps he wanted to use her to be a part of reaching her entire community. While she wasn't able to facilitate a DG at that time, we all thought she could help link us to the person of peace in the apartment complex who was open spiritually. We told her we'd be back each week, and she said, "That's great. Usually Christians just come through here, give people gospel tracts, and get out as quickly as they can." We were saddened by the reputation Christians had in that community and that many of them had run from danger rather than running right into the middle of it.

We helped Carol with her rent that month and have met with her a few more times to pray with her and talk about making disciples in that apartment complex. Without knowing it, Carol told us something in that first meeting that later proved to connect us with someone spiritually hungry. She said, "Do you guys see that apartment over there?"

We said, "The third one from the left?"

She replied, "Yes. That's a drug house. People come in and out all the time buying drugs."

We thanked her for the information, and my team partner and I decided to knock on that door first. We were nervous, but DMM training taught us that the hardest and scariest places often yield the greatest results. We wanted to go to the hardest place in the apartment complex first. When we knocked on the door, Billy answered.

Billy had just gotten out of prison. He was in his sixties. We told him we were praying in the area and wanted to know if we could pray for him in any way. He stepped outside and told us about getting out of prison and that we could pray for him to get back on his feet again. We prayed for him and then continued to chat with him. We learned that the apartment actually belonged to Billy's son, Joe. He was staying with Joe until he could get on disability and get his own place. My team partner and I exchanged glances when we realized it was the son, not the dad, who was the gatekeeper in that apartment complex . . . and possibly the chief drug dealer. We asked Billy if there were any needs we could meet for him and his family. He said they were okay, so we told him that we usually go out praying for people on Thursdays and that we'd come and see him again the next week.

Every Thursday morning, upon our arrival, Billy would see my car through his window and come outside to ask us to pray for him again. We almost never had a chance to make it to his door. He'd chat with us for a bit, and when we'd ask him if there was anything we could do for him, he'd never ask for anything but prayer.

One day as we went through our normal routine with Billy, he told us that his case worker had picked him up the day before and had taken him to a Bible study at a church nearby. We asked him how it went, and he said he loved it. He was really excited about it. He told us he wanted us to pray for him again, so we did.

Each time we met with Billy, we tried to ask him more about his son, Joe. He'd tell us that his son was on the wrong path and that he wanted us to pray for him to get back on the right path. I asked him once if we could go and pray for his son, and he said that his son didn't believe in God and probably wouldn't be open to that.

One day when we visited the complex, Billy didn't come right out, so we knocked on his door. Joe answered. He said his dad was in the shower and that he'd send him out when he was finished. Since this was the first time I had met Joe, I asked if we could pray for him. He turned us down but assured us that he'd send his dad out shortly.

Billy came out and had us pray for him as usual. I continued to ask more questions about his son. I knew that we looked out of place in that apartment complex, so I asked him one day, "Is Joe okay with us being here on Thursdays?"

Since I knew Joe was probably the gatekeeper, much like a tribal village chief, I wanted to know what he thought about our presence. Billy told us that his son was cool with us being there, so I asked him to reassure Joe that we're not the police and that we're just there to be a blessing to the apartment complex. Thankfully, it seemed as if he had already communicated that to his son, because anytime Joe saw that we were around praying for people, he never tried to get us to leave. But I figured it couldn't hurt to reinforce that fact.

One day, not long after, as we were praying for people, an SUV full of guys shouted out the window at us, "What's up, officers?" And then they peeled out of the parking lot. That's probably how we appeared to most people there since we had heard that officers were there all the time. But the people in the apartment complex who had gotten to know us realized we're not there to keep anyone in line, just to minister to people in Jesus' name.

We honestly believed that if someone gave us trouble Joe would come to our defense. Why? Because we made sure his dad was taken care of. Thanks to that relationship, it seemed we had Joe's blessing to be there.

Once this relationship had continued for some time, we finally asked Billy, "What would you think about us training you to lead a Discovery Group in your home? We can help you, Joe, his wife, and everyone else who comes through your door to learn to discover more about God by reading, obeying, and sharing his Word." Billy seemed interested in doing that but told us he didn't think Joe would feel the same way. Billy hesitated too, telling us he couldn't read very well.

Typically, if someone can't read, we help the person download the YouVersion Bible app on his or her phone, since it has an audio Bible connected to it. But that tactic doesn't always work since many low-income people don't have smartphones.

We talked to some of our friends overseas who minister to oral learners and asked what would be the best way to get Billy an audio version of the Bible. They showed us small speakers we could buy that receive SD cards. You can load the passages on the SD cards, and Billy could listen that way, then share with his group.

We told Billy, "How about this? We're going to get you a speaker that will play the Bible, and then we'll come on Thursdays and sit outside your apartment, listen to a passage with you, and teach you how to listen to God and obey him. How does that sound?" He said that sounded great.

Then I said, "Maybe you can invite some others from this same apartment complex to join us, and we can all listen to God's Word and obey it together." Billy agreed and mentioned some people he wanted to have come. We also had met several others in that apartment complex who were friends with Billy, and we thought they might be interested in joining in.

A week later we started the Discovery Group with Billy, and each week the group has grown. First it was just Billy. Then Billy and his neighbor Terry came. Then his other neighbor Tony came. Then his two other neighbors, Bob and Linda, came. Then others. In the first few weeks we taught the group the seven-question DBS process so they could eventually lead it on their own without our assistance. It is very exciting to watch the group begin to obey God together and share his Word with others.

We regularly cast vision to this Discovery Group that God wants to use them to reach their entire apartment complex. They often comment about how bad that area of town is and that they'd like to see it get better. We encourage them that God can use them to change the reputation of that area by leading people to become followers of Jesus. I'm beginning to sense a growing hunger in that group to be used by God to make many more disciples in that area.

Even though, as of this book's publication, Joe isn't receptive yet, we still have a sense that he may be a Saul who is going to have a Saul to Paul conversion and that he will be instrumental in seeing that apartment complex follow Jesus. Especially as he witnesses firsthand the radical transformation in his father's life. In fact, Billy told us recently that his son no longer claims to not believe in God and has actually started talking about God more. He was even supportive of one of his daughters getting baptized. We believe this is a direct result of the

We regularly cast vision to this Discovery Group that God wants to use them to reach their entire apartment complex.

transformation happening in his dad's life, and we rejoice that Joe is becoming more open spiritually.

Carol connected us to Billy. And Billy connected us to his oikos to begin a Discovery Group. We've recently had another person at that same apartment complex express interest in bringing family and friends together for a DG, so a second DG could begin soon in that same complex.

Our prayer is that these Discovery Groups might come to know Christ and be baptized together, leading to several churches being planted there and, eventually, the entire complex and neighborhood being transformed by Jesus.

Chapter 30

International

About fifteen years ago, while I was in college, my family took a class together called Perspectives,[1] which was all about catching God's heart for the nations. As a family, we had always supported missionaries, but this class encouraged us to be even more involved in what God is doing around the world. We just weren't sure how.

The class was transformational for our entire family; and soon after it ended, my mom was contacted by a friend and was asked if we would be interested in hosting an exchange student from Thailand named Kate. None of us really knew much about the exchange program, and we didn't have any friends who had done it before. Mom thought it might be an answer to our prayers about how to be more involved in the nations. She called the family together and asked if we wanted to host this student. We all felt that it could be a practical next step following Perspectives and could allow us to be more a part of what God is doing in the nations. Little did we know that the experience would change our lives forever.

Kate came to live with us, and our family fell in love with her. Kate was seventeen, and my sister, Kimberly, was eighteen. I was around twenty at the time and was living at home while going to college.

We found out early on that Kate was Buddhist. In fact, most people in her country were Buddhists. We didn't know much about Buddhism, so we asked Kate a lot of questions. What we realized is that many Buddhists don't know a lot about Buddhism either. It's just the religion of their country, and not everyone is fully devoted to it, especially the young people. They call themselves Buddhists, bow to the golden statues, visit the temples, take care of the monks, and all of that, but many young people aren't seriously committed to it.

Kate started going to church with us, and she was fascinated by the experience. In the youth group at our church she found kids who were on fire for Jesus. It wasn't that way with Buddhism in her country. She was drawn to the kids' love for her, their love for one another, and, most of all, their love for Jesus.

My sister and I started sharing Bible passages with Kate at home. It was unbelievable to us that she'd never heard most of this in her entire life. I was shocked that there could be people in the world who have never heard of Jesus or really knew any of the stories in the Bible.

Over time, Kate's experience with God was having a profound effect on her. One night Kate was at an event called "Saw You at the Pole," an evening rally following the "See You at the Pole" gathering that morning. There, she said she saw students worshiping Jesus with their hands in the air. I remember her telling us that she wanted what those students had. She also spoke about a powerful experience she had at an event in town where a former Muslim spoke about how he came to faith in Christ. She also got to visit with a Chinese man who had become a Christian, and that experience made her even more spiritually hungry. People started to ask Kate if she had become a Christian. Her regular response was, "No, but I'm about to."

One evening, during a long conversation with my mom and sister, Kate said, "I don't even know God, but I love him." My sister asked her if she believed in God now. She responded, "It seems unbelievable, but it's true." Later that night, Kate asked Mom how she could become a Christian. Mom shared the gospel with her and then encouraged her to go up to her room and talk to God about it. Mom didn't want Kate's parents to think we had pressured her to become a Christian, so she encouraged Kate to commit her life to Christ without our involvement. She came back out of that room a changed person, saved by Jesus and on fire to follow him. Kate was baptized soon after committing her life to Christ, and she and my sister chased after Jesus together.

My sister wrote a letter to Kate at the end of her exchange year. In the letter she described the transformation that she saw take place in Kate's life after she committed her life to Christ.

Kimberly wrote,

You told everything that breathed that you were a Christian. You were so proud to wear the Name of Jesus. I saw immediate change in you. Your outward appearance became so much more joyful, and your insides were bursting with good news. People were drawn to you. You immediately started serving in the church and going every time the doors were open. You wanted to tell your parents you were a Christian right away, but you knew they weren't supposed to call for another couple of weeks. So, at youth one night, we prayed and prayed that your parents would call. And so they did, as we were praying. God answers prayer! I remember at Hot Hearts you knew God was calling you to missions in Thailand. You weren't sure exactly what that meant, but you were ready to do whatever it took to obey. You want to win your nation for Jesus, and we're all right behind you. I have never had the privilege of being part of a more incredible salvation experience than yours. Praise God!

We were so sad to see Kate leave at the end of her exchange year, but we were thrilled to hear that when she returned home she led one of her sisters to Christ.

Years later, Kate married an American named Joel whom she met during her exchange year. They now have two beautiful children together. She continues to walk with Jesus, and God continues to use her to tell others about him.

Ten years later, when eLife was about six years old, one of our former youth ministers had just returned from a missions training center where he and his wife were preparing to go to the nations. Instead of going overseas immediately, they felt God leading them to come back to eLife and spend a few years mobilizing more people to go with them. Of course we were thrilled to have them back, but I didn't understand much about the mobilization process. Essentially, he told me about an organization called Launch Global, through which he'd planned to raise his financial support and that he'd come back on staff at eLife for free to help us excite people about the nations.[2]

Our church had always supported missionaries, but we definitely didn't have a process for sending our own people to the nations. Since we trusted him, we were excited to see what ideas he had for mobilizing people.

When he and his wife returned to work at our church, they moved into a rough apartment complex. The community was located near the local university where they heard many internationals lived. They could have afforded to live in a nice neighborhood, but they chose to move in among internationals to look for opportunities to get to know them and see them come to faith in Christ. After getting settled, he and his wife started meeting internationals and began to see DGs started among them. It wasn't long before they saw some of them trust in Christ. This was totally amazing and inspiring to watch.

We gave him free rein in our church to recruit whomever he wanted and so he started Phase One Goer Groups, where they would help people catch God's heart for the nations and then begin to pursue internationals who attended the local university.[3]

We have found that internationals are *so* receptive. They are in an unfamiliar place, a long way from home, and they're so eager for someone to reach out to them to develop a friendship. They are PIPSY, after all.

He and the people he recruited from our church began "fishing for people" (Matthew 4:19) among internationals, and the stories they told inspired our entire team.

I asked one of our staff members at the time, who was involved with this story, to share this incredible story in her own words.

> *We have found that internationals are so receptive.*

Two to three years ago, an Experience Life Mobilizer met Yin at an event on the Texas Tech campus. She sowed seeds with Yin and read the Bible with her a couple of times, but Yin wasn't very interested. Fast-forward a year or so later, Yin became interested in reading the Bible regularly with us (I was in Phase 2 at this time). We used DBS and went through "Creation to Christ" passages. Every week we could tell Yin was becoming more interested in Jesus. At one point she began texting us every day before she went to sleep—telling us that she was praying to Jesus and asking if there was anything we needed prayer for that we didn't mention that week. Every single day.

One day she called me and had been reading the Bible on her own. She wanted to tell me about the Tower of Babel. We realized that Yin is obedient to her "action step" every week we read the Bible, and she's always faithful to share what we read with her friends from back home in her country, even though they would not read the Bible with her yet. On top of obeying God's Word and sharing it, she was reading it without us and praying daily. Yin followed Jesus, and she had no idea!

We, along with our Phase 2 group, began praying for Yin six mornings a week at our Phase 2 prayer time, begging that Jesus would open her eyes to following him. After about three months of consistent reading, obeying, and sharing, Yin and some of our team members read John 3 together. Yin was mesmerized by Nicodemus's conversation with Jesus that we had to be born again and follow Jesus to have him. All Yin could say was, "I want to be born again and follow Jesus." So Yin followed Jesus that day. We then began reading scriptures about foundations of faith along with "Creation to Christ." Three months later, Yin came to us and said she wanted to be baptized. A couple weeks later, it happened in a bathtub. Ha!

Yin has been following Jesus for over a year now and has been multiplying her life in every area. She reads the Bible with other international students and employees she knows through Texas Tech, and she FaceTimes her friends and family back home to read the Bible with them, challenging them to know Jesus, obey, and share the same way we did. The Experience Life Mobilizer one day had a conversation with her about the unreached and showed her the stats on her home country. Yin's heart was broken to see that her country is considered reached because 3 percent of her country is considered evangelical. She had to come to America to learn about Jesus, so she is passionate about further reaching her own people group, so that people from her country don't have to travel thousands of miles to hear about Jesus the way she did.

Our church has heard so many stories like this one over

the years as we've reached out to internationals at the local university. Somewhere along the way, God really spoke to us about leading our church not to just pursue a vision of seeing West Texas come to Christ but also to pursue a vision of seeing Thailand come to Christ.

I was drawn to Thailand for obvious reasons. Kate was from there. Another international student from Thailand, Monsicha, lived with our family for six years after Kate left. She was pursuing her PhD at Texas Tech, and we became her home away from home. She became like a sister to me as well.

We sensed God leading us to mobilize and send as many workers from our church as we could to Thailand. At the time, we had about five thousand people coming to eLife, and we announced that we wanted to offer to God a "tithe" of our church to send to the nations. We started praying that five hundred people from eLife would be mobilized to the nations long-term. Since then, we've sent three long-term teams to Thailand and plan to send many more.

> Only about .5 percent of the people in Thailand are followers of Jesus.

As eLife began to prepare to send teams to Thailand, we were all convinced that we'd need to use the DMM strategy to reach the Thai people. Only about .5 percent of the people in Thailand were followers of Jesus, and there were millions of Thais who had never even heard of Jesus. We knew that doing church the "American" way by building buildings, raising money, hiring staff, putting on weekend services, and so on could not scale to reach millions. DMM was the solution. After all, DMM was being used in that part of the world to reach millions already.

I remember one day John, eLife's Executive Pastor, said to

me, "Isn't it sad that we can't encourage Thai pastors to look at what we are doing in America and imitate us? Clearly, we don't want them to do what we're doing. They need to reach millions. We're content with far less."

As a Senior Pastor of an American church, that really stung. I hated the notion that I had to make sure Thai pastors did *not* follow my example.

> *I hated the notion that I had to make sure Thai pastors did not follow my example.*

But it begged the question: Don't we need DMM in America too? Why does Thailand need DMM, but we're content in America not to see movements of God? We're content to build traditional American churches that reach very few people and grow mostly by transfer, often passing on the Word of God like its *just* information; and yet we want our Thai friends not to be content unless they execute a strategy that could reach their entire people group.

This was long before eLife began the DMM transition, but I remember thinking at that point that I wanted our church to model for our friends in Thailand what they should do. America has millions of people who are lost. I wondered why we would settle for less than a movement. It's not just Thailand that needs DMM. *We* need DMM. Why are American Christians satisfied without it? Why were we satisfied with a traditional American church when we could be "raising the sails" for a movement that could reach millions?

This conversation with John would be one of the key influences years later in our decision as a church to pursue DMM.

With our church now excited about the nations and mobilizing many people to be a part of the mission, I had to ask myself the question, *What's my role?* I had been preaching to our church that we're not all called to do the *same* thing but we're all called to do *some*thing. What was my "something"?

As I prayed about it, the thought came to mind, *Why not host another exchange student?* And even further, *Why not see if you can recruit many eLife families to host exchange students?*

Soon I thought about my family's incredible experience with Kate and Monsicha. If we encouraged others to take part in the exchange program, perhaps lifelong relationships would be built. Then our church would know many people in Thailand as a result of the program, and maybe those Thai families would even want to be involved with the long-term missionary teams we were sending out. Not only would this idea push the movement forward, it would provide support on the ground in Thailand to help our teams when they arrived. I felt this was from the Lord, and my wife and I began the process of trying to host a student.

As it turns out, I couldn't find any agency in town that was bringing Thai students to Lubbock. I contacted Kate's agency and some other agencies until I found one that was willing. They said they couldn't send students to us, though, until we had three international exchange coordinators in the area. I told them that I'd find the three. So my wife and I, and two other couples, became certified as IECs, which allowed the agency to start sending students here.

We knew our family would take a student; and after doing some recruiting, it turned out that nine other eLife families wanted to host students as well. We brought ten Thai exchange students to America that first year, and what happened was unbelievable! My family's story alone was life altering.

After looking at pictures and profiles of Thai students we could choose, our family picked a girl named Lukkaew.

Pronounced Luke-Gow. That was kind of hard for our family to say, so when we first spoke we asked if we could call her Lucy. She loved that name.

We were able to FaceTime with Lucy to begin getting to know her before she came to America. I remember meeting her, her mom, her dad, her brother, and her sister all via video chat. They were such a sweet family, and I could tell they were so excited for Lucy to come to America.

A month or so before Lucy was to come, while we were talking to her on the phone, she asked my wife and me, "Do you mind if I call you Mom and Dad?" That question melted our hearts. Of course she could! We knew in that moment that she would be an integral part of our family for the rest of our lives.

Lucy arrived in America. Although her English was good, it's easy for exchange students to get overwhelmed with all the English being spoken, and it takes a while to get acclimated. We immediately took her to a Thai food restaurant so she'd feel comfortable, and we started asking her questions to get to know her.

Lucy was friendly and a little shy. I've found that most Thais are the same way when you first meet them—they are typically very respectful and would never want to come across rude or overbearing.

We got Lucy settled into her new room, and she began school as soon as she arrived. She, like Kate, told us she was a Buddhist. This time I knew a little more about Buddhism. Lucy told us more about how her family practiced Buddhism, and she even showed me a picture of a worship/idol room that her family has in their own house. It's a small room with tons of golden statues that they can bow down to right in their house. Seeing the picture was heartbreaking, as you might imagine.

We didn't want to put any pressure on Lucy; but since our family read the Bible together in the evenings, we asked if she'd be interested in joining us. She always was.

My family and I didn't know anything about DMM when Kate was with us, so we just taught her the Bible and hoped she believed it. We didn't encourage her to bring her family along for the journey. Whereas with Lucy, in DMM fashion, we wanted her to "discover" these truths for herself through a DBS process and immediately begin sharing with her family so they could come along the journey as well.

We did DBS several nights a week as a family, and Lucy would read the passage with us. We'd all retell it in our own words, and then we'd ask the DBS questions. Lucy was always eager to participate. Because we knew she was new to the Bible, we started in Genesis 1 and went through our "Creation to Christ" sequence.[4] After reading about Adam and Eve, I asked Lucy, "Have you ever heard of them?" She replied, "No."

How is it that there are people in this world who don't know about Adam and Eve? She didn't know who Noah was either. Or Abraham. Or David. Or Peter. Or Paul. She had heard of Jesus only because she went to a private Catholic school in Thailand for a few years. But she knew hardly anything about Jesus or anything else in the Bible. It broke our hearts to think that there are so many people who haven't heard any of this. Jesus said the problem is that "the workers are few" (Matthew 9:37). Why have so few workers been willing to go? Should we go? Our family definitely started wrestling with all of this.

Over time, Lucy participated more and more in the DBS time. In fact, when we'd ask, "What should we *obey* from this passage?" Lucy would pick something to obey. When we'd ask, "Who should you *share* this with?" she would tell us someone she was going to share with. It was amazing! She was beginning to test out following Jesus long before she became a committed *follower* of Jesus.

After finishing the Old Testament passages and moving to the New Testament ones, we finally arrived at John 3 where Jesus talks about the need to be born again. We read the passage, asked the questions, and discovered that we all need a spiritual birthday in addition to a physical birthday. We need to be born again spiritually. I went around the table and asked everyone when their spiritual birthday was. My wife shared hers. Then my daughters shared theirs. I shared mine. And when it came to Lucy, she said, "My spiritual birthday happened when I came to live with your family."

Now, I was pretty sure she didn't fully understand what she was saying, but she was definitely seeking God. She had come to love Jesus as she met him through reading the Scriptures with us. To the extent that she understood, she was definitely trying to follow him. I could still tell, though, that there was reservation in her.

As the school year approached its end, I decided to take Lucy to dinner and have a serious spiritual conversation with her about whether or not she was ready to commit her life to Jesus. As we ate Thai food, I poured out my heart to Lucy about how much we loved her, why we had invited her to come and live with our family, and how we longed for the day she'd commit her life to Jesus. We told her we'd never put pressure on her, but that I was just curious to know where she felt like she was with Jesus. Lucy understood the gospel by this point, and she was having to count the cost of becoming a disciple of Jesus. After all, what would her family say? Would they kick her out? Would they want nothing to do with her anymore?

She said, "Dad, I've fallen in love with Jesus. I've loved reading the Bible with the family. I've learned so much. But, Dad, remember, my family is Buddhist. I grew up Buddhist. That's all I've ever known. I just don't think I'm ready to commit my life to Christ yet."

I was devastated. I tried not to let her see it, though. I told her I totally understood and that we'd always love her and be her family whether or not she ever became a Christian. We finished dinner, and a week or two later, as her exchange year ended, we hugged at the airport as Lucy left for home. Our family knew we had planted a seed. It was now time for someone else to water the seed and for God to make it grow (1 Corinthians 3:6–7).

When Lucy returned to Thailand, we all missed her. In fact, Lucy and our family became even closer when she was away—we texted with her and talked almost daily. I encouraged her to try out Nexus Church in Thailand sometime. We had become good friends with the pastors there. Lucy loved going to eLife while she was here, and I told her she'd like Nexus too, as it was similar to eLife. She said she would. I didn't know if she was serious, though, because I figured her family wouldn't want to take her.

You can imagine how surprised I was when a month or two later one of our short-term mission teams in Thailand took a picture of Lucy and her mom attending Nexus on Sunday morning.

I was ecstatic. I knew Lucy's mom had never even stepped foot in a church before. I started praying with all of my might that God would touch them while they were there. I was so excited that the entire service would be in Thai, their heart language. I couldn't imagine how powerful the gospel might sound to them in their own language!

At the end of the service, the pastor invited people who wanted to follow Jesus to come to the front and both Lucy *and* her mom went forward. The Nexus pastors took them aside into a room where they could talk to them further. One of the pastors shared more with them, told them how they could get more involved in the church, and prayed with them.

While I don't think Lucy and her mom were choosing to commit their lives to Christ at that point, they were definitely spiritually open and interested—and so they went forward. They were moved by the Holy Spirit through that service and they responded accordingly.

Then, about a month later, I got one of the best phone calls of my life. I even remember where I was. I was playing soccer in our front yard with my daughters. The call was from Lucy. I answered, and she was so excited.

She said, "Daddy, Daddy!"

"What?" I responded.

She said, "I'm a Christian. I know I am. I committed my life to Christ, and I want to follow him forever. I want my country to know about him, Daddy! Daddy! I'm so excited! I'm a Christian!"

I about fell over.

Lucy and I had continued to read the Bible together after she left our home, and between her experience with our family, her time at Nexus Church, her time reading the Bible, and perhaps some Christian Thais she met, she was brought to faith in Christ.

Since then, we've continued to talk almost daily. We share powerful Bible verses with each other. She's begun sharing even more with her family. One day Lucy sent me a screenshot of something she had sent to her family. She said that each morning her mom will send out a picture of Buddha to the family, wishing them good luck for that day. She responded to her mom with a picture of herself smiling and the message, "Hello Tuesday. God loves everyone. Amen!" written on the picture.

Lucy's family is likely skeptical, but I know they've observed transformation in her life. I continue to encourage her to share with them so that she might see all of them come to know Jesus eventually too.

Will you "go out among the lost" in places where internationals are and consider inviting them into your home? Perhaps if you do, you'll get to be a part of "making disciples of *all* the nations" (Matthew 28:19, italics mine).

Chapter 31

Prisoner

One of our goals early on at eLife was to start ten campuses in ten years. We were a multisite church and wanted to try to add a new campus each year to reach out into a new area. As we were praying about where to plant these various campuses, I saw an article in *Forbes* magazine that bothered me. The article was published in 2011, and it was titled "America's Most Dangerous Cities."[1] I was horrified to read that my town, Lubbock, Texas, was listed as the sixth most dangerous city in America.[2] How could that be? The list was created by comparing the total number of violent crimes per 100,000 residents in a city. Lubbock had 808 violent crimes for every 100,000 residents, landing us at the number six spot.

I initially thought, *What do they mean by violent crimes? Lubbock isn't that violent—is it?* Violent crime was defined as murder, nonnegligent manslaughter, forcible rape, robbery, and aggravated assault. I could hardly believe that crimes such as these were happening in my own backyard.

The only way 808 violent crimes would possibly go to zero was if people's hearts were changed. Jesus is the One who changes hearts. And he sends out his church to tell people this good news!

I knew eLife had to do something. Law enforcement could only do so much. Rehab facilities could only do so much. Community organizations could only do so much. These people needed Jesus.

The article bothered me so much that I started praying about it regularly and thinking about how eLife could be part of the solution to this problem. I reasoned that the only way to solve the problem was to get to know the people who were *part* of the problem. We had to get to the people who could likely become part of the 808. We had to connect with the people likely to commit violent crimes to prevent this from happening in the future. That begged the question, "How do we get to them?"

Then the lights went on. We had to go to the Lubbock jail.

Many of the people who commit violent crimes, namely the 808, end up in jail for lesser crimes first. Perhaps we could intersect them in the jail. We could meet them at their lowest point, introduce them to Jesus, and provide a community in jail in which they could begin to follow Jesus. Then, when they got out of jail for the lesser crime, they'd be far less likely to commit another, more violent crime. In fact, as Jesus changes their lives, chances are, many of them will never commit any kind of crime again. It soon became clear that there was a tangible way to get that 808 number to drop to zero.

We knew we needed to get into the jail. But didn't have any contacts who could help, so I wasn't sure how to get in.

I kept praying about it; and a few years later, I happened to meet a man from the sheriff's department after church one Sunday. I asked him what he thought about us starting a church in the jail—an actual eLife campus. He said he thought it was a great idea but that we'd need to talk to the chaplain at the jail.

We had lunch with the chaplain a few times, and he thought the church was a good idea too. There were people who were doing ministry at the jail and having a Bible study here and there; but to our knowledge, there was not a functioning church in the jail.

Right around this time, the chaplain told us in one of our meetings that the warden had actually talked to him about wanting to build a baptism tank in the jail. We thought that might be an affirmation of what we were sensing God was leading us to do.

Everything ended up coming together, and in 2014, we launched our first Freedom Campus in the Lubbock County Detention Center.[3] God moved so powerfully through that campus that other jails in the area were asking us to come out and start a Freedom Campus in their facility as well.

So many of the men and women in these facilities are at the lowest point in their lives, which can produce a great deal of spiritual hunger in someone. When you ask them if they want prayer, it seems that everyone does. When you challenge them to obey Jesus in some way, it seems that everyone wants to obey. When you give them an opportunity to commit their lives to Christ, it seems that everyone wants to make this decision.

I joke with our staff that if I wasn't the Lead Pastor, I'd want to be a Freedom Campus Pastor. The hunger for God at our Freedom Campuses is simply electric. It's hard to explain the feeling you get when you go in there to those who haven't been.

After our ten-year anniversary, and the transition of our church to DMM, we started doing things differently at our Freedom Campuses. Instead of just trying to draw men to a worship service on the weekend, we started casting vision to them and training them to be disciple makers. We'd suggest to them that instead of bringing their friends in their pods with them to church, why not "go out among the lost" in their pods and start Discovery Groups? Perhaps those Discovery Groups would become churches, and perhaps people in those churches would catch a vision to go back to some of their rough neighborhoods upon their release to make disciples and start churches there too.

DMM provided a complete shift in how we saw our ministry in the jail. Instead of bringing them to us, which wouldn't be scalable, we wanted to train them and send them out. If we did that, our influence would extend far outside of the jail. Disciples could be made and churches could be started all across the nation when those currently in jail were able to move back home.

DMM provided a complete shift in how we saw our ministry in the jail.

We had such a strong interest in the DMM training that we recently started seven or eight training groups with inmates interested in becoming disciple makers. We still have our weekend gatherings, but we're now using those gatherings to find the spiritually hungry men who are willing to start groups.

Meet Henry.

Henry caught the vision to be a disciple maker and go through our DMM training. The first few weeks of the training cover Elements #1 and #2 of the 7 Ongoing Elements in

Movements. Element #1 is "Focus on God's Word," where you learn to read, obey, share, and start new DGs by using the seven-question DBS process. Element #2 is "Multiply Extraordinary Prayer," where you learn to grow in your prayer life and cast vision to others to do the same.

Henry and the others in his training were challenged to go back to their pods and begin implementing the training. Soon after, Henry and one of the other inmates started a DG in pod 4D. This was done without assistance from us. We trained them and served as their coach but let them do the "work of the ministry" (Ephesians 4:12).

One Sunday morning, in the worship gathering, Henry stood and shared about how the DG was growing and their prayer times as a group were very powerful. He said there was only one problem. They couldn't seem to keep their group meeting time under four hours!

Henry's group meets every single day in that pod, and lives are being transformed. They're so hungry, and they just can't get enough of hearing and obeying God's Word and praying with one another. When I told Stan this story, he told me it reminded him of the early church, which met many times a week, not just once. In fact, Stan said one key hindrance to growth in movements is if the church gets the idea that they are only "supposed" to meet once a week.

Henry told us that he was getting out of jail soon but didn't want to see the group come to an end. He said he had trained two other guys to take over the group. In addition, he told us that he planned to start another DG when he left the jail.

Dave is much like Henry.

Dave attends a DG that was started in his pod. There are

about six to eight inmates in the group. They do the seven-question DBS process when they meet in order to read, obey, and share the Bible together. People in that group often talk about how Dave has become a spiritual leader among them. They talk about how he has helped them and how he keeps them on the right track.

Dave has been challenged to start new DGs as well. Recently, Dave started a second-generation DG in his cell with the other inmates. They get together and do the same seven-question DBS process. Dave also began coaching them to start new groups. As a result, Ivan and Jimmy, two guys in that second-generation DG, each started a third-generation DG in their respective cells. They gather together; use the DBS process; and read, obey, and share together. Dave has talked about staying connected with our team when he gets out of jail so he can start more groups with the people in his relational network. We have several streams of second-generation DGs in the jail, and at least one stream of third-generation DGs.

> We have several streams of second-generation DGs in the jail, and at least one stream of third-generation DGs.

After another pod had gone through the DMM training, many of the men started "going out among the lost" in their pod and trying to figure out how to serve the men there. They were looking for a person of peace who might receive the gospel and then pass it on to the rest of the pod, and they had learned in their training that one way you find potential persons of peace is by serving people and meeting needs.

To understand what they did, you need a little insight into life inside of a jail. Obviously, the facility feeds the inmates three meals a day, but anything between those meals, like snacks, has to be purchased by the inmates. They get the money to purchase those items through family members and friends putting money on their "books." When they do this, they're able to purchase commissary items. Commissary items are highly treasured in the jail.

Around Thanksgiving and Christmas, the men knew that many of the guys in the pods didn't have money on their "books" to buy something special to eat for those holidays. As a result, the guys who went through the DMM training pooled their money and bought commissary items to feed the entire pod of sixty-four men. They were able to share these specialty items with their pod and pray over all of them. They used the miracle question, "If God could do a miracle in your life, what would you have him do?" to pray for people. Then they prayed for these men. If God answers that prayer, the person being prayed for would know it's a miracle.

As the men get out of the jail, we invite them to a transition group to help them get back on their feet again. The group originally met in the house of the Freedom Campus Pastor, but now it meets in the lobby of a hotel that has had a reputation for being the largest dope and prostitution house in Lubbock. Many of the same guys had been there before for the wrong reasons. Now they meet there to read God's Word, pray together, and share with the people who happen to be there. They regularly baptize people in the hotel swimming pool, and the new general manager has given them free rein of the hotel because he believes in the vision. In fact, when our team originally asked him if we could meet in that hotel and baptize people who followed Christ, he said, "Yes, you definitely can, but only if you'll baptize me first."

Since the inception of the first Freedom Campus, we've started two more Freedom Campuses: one is in a Texas prison facility, and another one is in a drug rehabilitation facility. Both have seen extraordinary things happen, just as our campus in the Lubbock jail did. The Freedom Campuses have seen so much life transformation, and now, as we begin to train the inmates in a DMM approach, we believe our community can have a fighting chance of reducing drastically the 808.

Chapter 32

Sick

Jesus told his disciples in Matthew 10 and Luke 10 that when they entered a new area, they were to heal the sick and announce that the Kingdom of Heaven was near.

In movements around the world, one way church planters are able to gain access into a new area is by asking if they can pray for the sick people in that area. When God heals someone, it gets the community's attention, and all of a sudden people are open to listening to the message about such a powerful God.

If you were to look more closely at the more than 650 active movements today, most leaders would acknowledge that miracles have been very influential in the rapid multiplication of churches they are seeing.[1] In fact, in many movements, more than half of the persons of peace are found through miracles. I hear it often described this way: many people first come to know Jesus as Healer and later come to know him as Savior.[2] It's not uncommon for a missionary from the United States to begin his or her work overseas being skeptical about miracles, only to be convinced quickly that God still uses them to confirm the message of the gospel.

> *Miracles have been very influential in the rapid multiplication of churches.*

As miracles are happening in movements all over the world, our teams began to pray that they would happen here too. We learned from several movement resources to ask the miracle question that I've already referenced throughout this book: *If God could do a miracle in your life, what would you have him do?* Then we'd pray immediately for that miracle.

In Beyond's six CPM steps, healing and miracles are so common in movements that they list this as CPM step 4.[3]

This is so important to us that some of our teams have gone to hospitals to pray for the sick. One team started going to the waiting room in a local hospital and asking people if they could pray for their sick family member or friend. Often they would announce to the whole waiting area that they'd like to pray for anyone who was open to it. Many people would jump up, eager to be prayed for, so they'd form a big circle right there, hold hands, and begin praying for people.

A second team soon began going to the same hospital looking for sick people to pray for. They would interact with family members standing outside of hospital rooms and let them know they were available to pray for their loved one if they wanted prayer. Several families even invited the team into the room to pray with the patient.

On one occasion, while doing this, one of the teams got lost while trying to get back to the lobby. Somehow they ended up in the waiting area of the burn unit, which was a restricted area. They talked to a family sitting in the waiting area, and a family member mentioned that they were there for his uncle, who was in the burn unit after suffering major burn wounds in a recent accident. The family asked if our team would go and pray for him.

Because the area was restricted and only family was allowed to enter, a family member pressed the button to get in and convinced the nurses to allow our team to come in to pray with the patient. They knocked on the uncle's door, and more family members were sitting at his bedside. Our team mentioned that some of the other family members had sent them to pray and asked if that would be okay. The family members said yes.

The burn victim was in his sixties, and he had been injured a few days earlier in some kind of grease fire in his kitchen. The fire resulted in major burn wounds on his chest and arms, so bad that he couldn't move his arms. His wife told our team that it was the most horrifying thing she'd ever seen. She had walked into the house to find her husband on fire.

One of the members of the team, John, said, "I believe Jesus Christ has the power to heal you, and we'd like to pray for you. Is that okay?" The man nodded his head. They gently put their hands on the bandages on his arms and started praying. John said as they were praying, they had a sense that their prayers were effective and were making a difference for this man. After the prayer was finished, John asked him, "How does it feel?"

The man lifted up his arms and started moving them around, and the family collectively gasped. He hadn't been able to do that before. Then he raised his arms above his head, and family members began crying right there by his bedside. They were so thankful to the team and told them they were the best visitors they'd had. Right after, the team had the chance to pray in the lobby with more of the man's family. Some of them weren't religious, but John could tell they were moved by the prayers.

Can you imagine how open the family was to spiritual things at this point? They had just witnessed the power of God! Praying for the sick can result in open hearts, eager to hear the good news about the Kingdom.

Praying for the sick can result in open hearts, eager to hear the good news about the Kingdom.

On another occasion this same team was prayer walking in a very difficult and dangerous part of town. They had decided that they wouldn't approach anyone for prayer unless someone engaged them in conversation as they walked by. They crossed one particular house, said hello, and waved to the people in the front yard who asked them what they were doing. They told them they were prayer walking and asked if there was any way they could pray for them. They said yes and were eager to have someone pray for them. They were taken to meet a nine-year-old girl named Jazea who was struggling with severe asthma. She had to go to the doctor on a regular basis for breathing treatments because the asthma was so bad. Our team said they'd like to pray for her, and they did.

A few weeks later, when they went back to check on Jazea, the family was ecstatic to see them. The family eagerly told our team that Jazea had not had to go back to the doctor since the team prayed for her. Jazea had told her family that she felt different ever since she was prayed for. The family believed that God had touched Jazea in response to prayer.

Just down the block from this family, our team met someone else named Don, who was sitting in his front yard when the team passed by. As Don engaged them in conversation, the team noticed that he had bandages on both legs from his knees down to his feet. They asked what was wrong with his legs, and he told them he was struggling with diabetes and had developed painful sores all over his feet. They asked Don if they could pray for him and he said yes. They prayed for complete healing in Jesus' name.

When the team returned to check on Don a few weeks later, he walked out of his house to them with no bandages on his legs or his feet. And they noticed he wasn't limping as he had been before. He said he was better, the sores were healing, and he believed he had been healed in answer to their prayers.

Remember Billy and and his son Joe from chapter 29? One day when Billy approached our team for prayer, he told us we could pray for him because he was "hearing voices." Based on his description of what was going on, several of our team members sensed there could be some demonic involvement there. One of our team members asked him, "Did any of them tell you their name?" He said no. We laid hands on Billy and immediately began to pray for deliverance from the "voices" and any demonic powers that had influence over him. We prayed passionately for the "voices" to leave in Jesus' name. Honestly, I went to a Baptist seminary, so I had never been a part of anything like this before. It was powerful!

After we prayed for Billy, I asked him, "How do you feel now?"

He responded, "Much better."

When our team "goes out among the lost," and we ask people how we can pray for them, we typically ask two more questions after praying: (1) Do you have any needs in your life right now, or do you know of any needs in this area? And (2) Is anyone in your family sick, or do you know anyone in this area who is sick?

The reason we ask the first question is because we're looking for means of access into the area. By meeting needs we establish a reason for being there and hope that God leads us to the person of peace. If they tell us of needs in the area, we begin to pray about how we could possibly serve those people and meet those needs.

The reason we ask the second question is because we are constantly looking for opportunities to pray for the sick and see them healed. This opens a door for the gospel to be shared with a whole relational network as people are amazed by God's power. When people tell us about the sick individuals in that area, we make it a point to visit them immediately to pray.

Praying for the sick has opened up many doors for us as we've sought to make disciples and plant churches. Do you know who's sick around you? Have you gone to them and prayed for them? Perhaps Jesus would heal them in response to prayer and give you a captive audience eager to become his disciples!

Chapter 33

Tentmaking

When our church transitioned to DMM we began to cast vision for ordinary people with normal jobs to begin to see themselves as disciple makers and church planters. I feared what some people must've been thinking as I was casting that vision. Something like, *Easy for you to say. You're paid by the church. Of course you can plant churches and make disciples. But not me. I have a job. I have to work. There's no way I could do that.*

I desperately wanted to overcome that objection for the sake of the mission. If we were going to see a movement, businessmen and -women would have to believe they could be church planters too, even if they work a regular nine-to-five job.

In our context the idea of "church planting" can be misunderstood. We think immediately of planting an American church and the time, money, and energy that it takes. In DMM, church planting is not the same thing as what we did in the first ten years at eLife. It's not planting a typical American church that takes well over forty hours per week to work on. If that were the case, hardly anyone could do it.

We're talking about rabbit church planting or simple church planting.[1] You can do that with a normal full-time job. It doesn't take forty hours per week. Or even thirty. Or even twenty. If it took that long, the apostle Paul couldn't have done it, since he was working too. He wouldn't have had the time to plant an American church and carry a full-time job. In DMM, the kinds of churches we're planting aren't churches with expensive buildings, budgets, and staff. They are simple churches focused on making new disciples and starting new churches down to the fourth generation and beyond. And that's a good thing, because the average American church, even with all its bells and whistles, is struggling to reach people, as we've already shown. We're planting the kind of churches that can reproduce quickly. We're planting book-of-Acts-style churches like the kind reaching millions all over the world.

Paul wouldn't have had the time to plant an American church and carry a full-time job.

But, again, someone might still argue that it's easy for me to talk about church planting because I'm paid by a church. And that's a fair point.

I began to feel the Lord convicting me to lead by example. If I'm going to say you can be a businessman and a church planter, then I need to be a businessman and a church planter. Just like Paul. At times Paul ran a tentmaking business to provide for his needs so the churches wouldn't have to pay him.

> Then Paul left Athens and went to Corinth.
> There he became acquainted with a Jew named
> Aquila, born in Pontus, who had recently arrived
> from Italy with his wife, Priscilla. They had left

Italy when Claudius Caesar deported all Jews
from Rome. Paul lived and worked with them,
for they were tentmakers just as he was. Each
Sabbath found Paul at the synagogue, trying to
convince the Jews and Greeks alike. (Acts 18:1–4)

Notice that Paul went to Corinth to preach the gospel, but he worked a normal job as a tentmaker with Aquila and Priscilla. Then on Saturdays, and at other times, he'd be out among the lost trying to "convince" people to follow Jesus.

I have never coveted anyone's silver or gold or
fine clothes. You know that these hands of mine
have worked to supply my own needs and even
the needs of those who were with me. And I have
been a constant example of how you can help
those in need by working hard. (Acts 20:33–35)

In this passage, Paul expressed to the Ephesian elders that no one had to give him any money while he was with them. He worked to supply his own needs. Not only that, he supplied the needs of his friends who were with him. He did this to act as an example, showing how to help those in need by working hard. Paul worked hard, as so many Americans do, and he was still one of the most effective church planters of all time.

What then is my pay? It is the opportunity to
preach the Good News without charging anyone.
(1 Corinthians 9:18)

Paul had the right to be paid for preaching the gospel. He was a traveling missionary, and it would've been difficult for him to hold down a job like someone who stayed in one place. Even still, he would often work when he traveled so as not to be a burden to anyone. He wanted to preach the gospel free of charge.

These verses, among others, were the ones that convinced me I needed to lead by example also. I've started working on a side business to generate income so that I can come off the church payroll. I'm still planning to put in full-time hours at the church, but I wanted to earn my income from the side business so the church wouldn't have to pay me.

As of this writing, I'm not completely off the church payroll, but I'm making progress. I've asked the elders to cut a significant amount of money from my church salary that I plan to derive from my business. As the business continues to prosper, I plan to keep asking them to make cuts until I'm down to nothing. I'm excited, Lord willing, to eventually work in the ministry completely for free.

Paul was a tentmaker in the New Testament so he could "preach the gospel free of charge." I feel led to do what Paul did. Like Paul, I want to be a businessman and a church planter to provide an example that you can do both. That's critical for our vision of reaching a million people in the next ten years.

Lee, our former Downtown Campus Pastor, felt the same way. After helping our church make the DMM transition, he knew he needed to resign as the Campus Pastor, take a normal job, and become a businessman and a church planter. He was so sold on the DMM strategy that he didn't feel that he could derive an income from a traditional church anymore. He said that reading *The Great Evangelical Recession* was one of the things that "ruined his love affair with the traditional model of the American church." Learning that the American church was in trouble, and also experiencing firsthand how disciple making had taken a back seat to weekend productions, caused him to "contemplate the way he had invested the majority of his adult life as a pastor." Lee said that he went from absolutely loving the way our church functioned and feeling like he had his dream job to suddenly feeling discontent and that he couldn't do it any longer. He felt that the Lord wanted him to invest significantly less energy on the weekend at big corporate gatherings and place disciple making at the forefront of what he did on a daily basis.

Lee said, "The DMM approach sets you up to be a more intentional disciple maker in all aspects of your life. Whether you're in the workplace or in your neighborhood, every encounter and every location is now viewed as an opportunity to build a relationship, start a DG, and plant a church. It's changed everything for me and my family, and we aren't looking back."

Lee was compelled to lead businessmen and -women who were hungry to make disciples and plant churches by example in becoming a businessman himself. He is currently on a DMM church planting team, which meets in his home, and they are aiming to plant many churches in the days to come. He is currently working full-time in the business world, and he loves it. He's around the lost all day long, whereas as a paid pastor, that's more difficult. He's able to influence those around him to see themselves as disciple makers and church planters as well.

I want to be clear that I'm not saying this is for everyone. Most of eLife's staff members are paid. However, I had the personal conviction through reading Scripture to live my life this way. Lee did as well. And if you feel that conviction, please know that you're not alone and that it can be done.

If *only* full-time paid ministry workers see themselves as church planters, then we will not make it to the 1,000,000. Everyone has to see him- or herself as a church planter, no matter where he or she works. But it's important that we have among us some examples of people who both work in business and are also devoted to making disciples and seeing churches planted.

> If only full-time paid ministry workers see themselves as church planters, then we will not make it to the 1,000,000.

My role in leading eLife has not changed at all. I'm hoping that in five to ten hours per week I can make all I need from my business to provide for my family so I can devote as much time to the movement as possible.

Chapter 34

Weekend Planning

P rayer. Testimony. Training. Those are the three primary
elements in our new weekends that are leveraged for
DMM, which I also talked about in chapter 7. I want to take a
few minutes to explain what this looks like practically.

Each campus plans its service independently, so I'll share
how our Southwest Campus planned its service on one of
the most powerful weekends we've had to date. Typically, the
Southwest Campus team will meet on Tuesdays to plan the
following weekend. Because we're trying to "multiply extraordinary prayer" as we raise DMM sails for movement, they'll
spend the first hour of their meeting in prayer. They'll ask
God to guide the preparation of the service and to move powerfully that weekend (Acts 4:31). After praying, they'll start to
talk about the upcoming weekend.

We usually provide the "training" part of the weekend
centrally, which means our central staff has planned the series
and has chosen speakers weeks ahead of time. Right now, as a
church, we're going through the book of Acts. We wanted to
spend a lot of time in Acts in this season because Acts describes
what we're hoping will happen in our church and in our region.

Like I mentioned before, one of my DMM coaches said, "When people ask what DMM is, I basically tell them that we're asking God that the book of Acts would happen again in our day!" People seem to understand that, since Acts is the powerful story of the early church and the rapid advancement of the gospel.

Our Southwest Campus team knew that Ty, our Abernathy Campus Pastor, was doing the "training" that weekend on Acts 5:12–16. Remember, DMM is based on obedience-based discipleship, so *training* is much more important than just teaching.

Ty had several weeks in which to prepare his training on that Scripture passage. Each of our trainings revolves around the DBS questions. This is common in movements around the world that have a training element in their gatherings. As our speakers prepare their outlines, the sections usually look like this:

- Introduction
- Read the passage
- Retell the passage
- Ask:
    - What does the passage teach us about God?
    - What does it teach us about people?
    - What should we obey in response?
    - Who should we share with?
- Personal story of obeying and sharing the passage
- Conclusion

By formatting the "training" this way, it keeps the DBS process in front of our church. Not only are we focusing on reading, obeying, and sharing in small groups, we're also focusing on those things when we get together in a larger group. The training shouldn't be about knowledge acquisition, as sermons often are, but about hearing and obeying the Word of God immediately. Because we're emphasizing immediate obedience, we keep the trainings relatively short. Typically they run about ten to twelve minutes.

In the first ten years of eLife, the sermon could be anywhere from thirty to thirty-five minutes. That's because it was focused primarily on knowledge acquisition. When we transitioned to DMM, and subsequently moved to an immediate obedience focus, the trainings needed to be shorter. We've found that the longer the trainings run, the more difficult it is for people to obey.

Think about it like this: Imagine you're starting a new job, and your boss is training you on how to use the company's

> We've found that the longer the trainings run, the more difficult it is for people to obey.

proprietary software. If he or she gives you a thirty-minute presentation on the ins and outs of the software and then expects you to be fully proficient in using it, you'll be completely overwhelmed and, likely, unable to perform. But that has nothing to do with you or your level of intelligence! It's because the presentation gave you way too many things to remember and apply that you've never done before. You've experienced information overload.

An effective boss or trainer should show you one or two things at a time, letting you give those things a try and ask questions along the way until you get it. This is the MAWL approach, the same concept I introduced in chapter 17. Remember: Model. Assist. Watch. Launch.

Just like my dad teaching me to drive a stick shift, if someone dumps a bunch of information on you, he or she is setting you up to fail if the goal is for you to implement it. Now, if the goal isn't to implement it but just to be impressed by it and informed about it, that person can talk as long as he or she wants and it won't matter. You're not expected to do anything with it anyway.

Do you see where I'm going? When sermons go on and on, it is likely that the preacher is not expecting you to implement it, just be fascinated by it. And, in my opinion, that's the modern American sermon and is indicative of the American church model. Preachers wonder why people aren't living out or applying what they're preaching. But they need to be open to the fact that it's because the whole format of a lecture-type sermon is built to transfer information, not to help people obey. Remember, Jesus said we're supposed to teach people to obey (Matthew 28:20), not just be fascinated or intrigued.

If a preacher really wants you to implement what he or she is teaching, then the preacher will briefly tell you one thing to focus on and spend the rest of the time helping you implement it. That's how our strategy has shifted as we head toward the million goal, and that's why the trainings are shorter. We strive for obedience, not knowledge acquisition.

> *When sermons go on and on, it is likely that the preacher is not expecting you to implement it, just be fascinated by it.*

As Ty prepares his message, he'll make sure that after he talks briefly about what he discovered in the passage, he gives a strong challenge to *obey* and *share*. These are two of the key elements at the heart of DMM that we often miss in the American church.

That weekend, when Ty got up to train, he gave a brief introduction, read his passage, retold his passage in his own words, shared some things he learned about God and people, and then challenged us to share immediately what we learned and commit to obey.

Acts 5:12–16 tells how the apostles were performing miracles among the people and the people were being drawn to Jesus. During the training, Ty's challenges for the week were:

> **OBEY:** Go out among the lost for one hour this week.
>
> **SHARE:** Pray for someone who needs healing and share Acts 5:12–16 with that person.

As you can see, there is an emphasis on immediate obedience and sharing. The Bible is not a collection of books that are just meant to be learned. It's a collection of books meant to be obeyed.[1]

The Southwest Campus team had seen the outline of Ty's upcoming weekend training when they arrived at their weekly meeting on Tuesday, and they began to build their service around it. They planned for the service to start off with a song, followed by our Youth Pastor welcoming everyone and casting vision for what we were doing that day. After that, Ty was going to come up for ten to twelve minutes for his training on Acts 5. Then they had planned a ten-minute testimony time after the message that our Associate Campus Director would lead.

Testimonies have become one of the major elements in our weekends. During this particular testimony section, the Southwest Campus team decided to give people the opportunity to come up to an "open mic" and share stories of how God has healed them or healed someone they know. This would give the congregation greater confidence to obey the challenge, because as they pray for people they remember that God still answers prayer. The hope was that they would recall the answers to prayer they had heard during the testimony section of the service. This testimony time would further drive home the training Ty did and would end up being much more effective in helping people implement the training than if he had simply continued transferring information for another twenty minutes.

After people shared testimonies of healing for a while, the team planned to have a ten-minute prayer time. They would invite people in the room who were in need of healing to stand; then others would gather around them, place a hand on their shoulder, and pray for them. In this way, they were able to practice Ty's challenge before they even left the room. The team was preparing the people to pray for others by showing them how to do it right then and there.

Following this section, the team planned to have a worship set with a gospel presentation between the songs to invite people to commit their lives to Christ there on the spot. This allows for another act of immediate obedience.

I'd like to draw your attention to a couple of things here. First, notice how many people are involved. As I mentioned in chapter 8, one of our values in this new decade has been to have many people using their gifts during the service, not just one or two. In the first ten years, and in most churches, a preacher and a worship team use their gifts during the service, and that's about it. This seems counter to the gatherings of the New Testament church, where many people participated.

We wanted to adopt that model at eLife. If you come to our church now, you'll see many people coming on the stage to pray, share a testimony, or train.

Second, notice that the testimony and prayer sections are interactive. People come to the front to share. People stand for prayer. Others gather around them. In the first ten years the

If you come to our church now, you'll see many people coming on the stage to pray, share a testimony, or train.

congregation would basically sit through the service. In our new decade, we're encouraging everyone to get involved. We want our services to be highly participatory, much like the early church services described in 1 Corinthians 14:26–33.

Third, the prayer and testimony sections serve to emphasize the challenge of the message and prepare people to obey and share. Typically, there is no time in a service for extended prayer and testimony sections because the sermon is so long, but we've found that prayer and testimony make it much more likely people will actually obey and share the training rather than just listen and be intrigued by it.

Fourth, while our services revolve around prayer, testimony, and training, the format is different every weekend. Each campus team is welcome to format their weekend service in the way they think would be most powerful for the people who attend their campus. Believe it or not, sometimes we'll only stay in the building for ten minutes or so and then dismiss everyone to leave and implement the training immediately. For example, we did this when we talked about prayer walking. We trained on it for a few minutes and then sent everyone out to prayer walk their neighborhoods with their families. It was extremely powerful; many families had never experienced that together before!

To summarize, we *train* people to obey and share the Word of God, and then we *pray* that God will help us do this and share *testimony* of how it's happening in our lives. We believe this is the best way we've found to "teach [people] to obey," as Jesus told us to do in the Great Commission.

I attended the worship gathering described in this chapter with my family, and it was one of the most powerful meetings of the entire year. Hearing Ty passionately lead us to obey the Word of God was moving. Seeing people come up in tears and share testimonies of how God healed them was so powerful! Watching my daughters lay hands on people who were sitting around us and pray for them to be healed was breathtaking! How did we miss this all these years? It's amazing when everyone participates! It felt like Acts 4:31, which says, "After this prayer, the meeting place shook, and they were all filled with the Holy Spirit. Then they preached the word of God with boldness."

Prayer and testimony have been instrumental time and time again in revivals of the past! So, I wonder, why aren't they more prominent in American worship services?

Chapter 35

Ty

S peaking of Ty, I want you to hear more of his story. Ty is currently the Campus Pastor at our Abernathy Campus. God has done extraordinary things in Abernathy, Texas, since that campus launched, and we believe that with the new DMM vision their best days are still ahead. I think that many of you will identity with Ty's church background and also with his struggle on the journey into DMM. Here is how Ty explains his story:

———∞∞∞———

I grew up in the small West Texas town of Abernathy. My community, located in the Bible belt, had a population of about three thousand people, but there were plenty of churches to choose from, about thirteen in fact. I was raised in a strong Christian family. I "committed my life to Christ" and was baptized at the age of eight, was a leader in my youth group, went to summer camps every year, taught a Sunday school class, and so forth. Basically, any way you could be involved in a church, I was.

As I graduated from high school, I enrolled in college at Texas Tech University and began looking for a church to call home. I tried what I knew—every Baptist church in town—and while there was nothing wrong with the churches I tried, none felt like the right fit. I heard about this church that was meeting in a skating rink called Experience Life, right down the road from my apartment. It had to be a cult, right? My small-town, traditional mind couldn't comprehend it. But I was curious, so I tried it.

From the first Sunday I attended, I fell in love. It was a vibrant, growing, hip new church that was attracting people from all walks of life. It was so different from anything I was used to because they were reaching lost people. I began to volunteer; and with my then girlfriend, and now wife, joined a small Bible study group. I met some of my best friends to this day. I was getting to be a part of thousands of lives being changed. In a two-weekend span, I saw more than six hundred people go public with their faith and get baptized. I thought, *What have I been missing my whole life?* This was it.

Experience Life decided to launch a new campus in the downtown area, across town from where I lived, and I chose to be a part of that volunteer launch team. While all this was exciting, my real-world life was pretty miserable. I worked in a sales job simply for a paycheck. I hated it.

I thought, *There has to be something God has out there for me other than this.* Little did I know God was preparing me for the ministry.

An intern position came open at our Downtown Campus. I stepped into that role, and through a series of events, lots of prayer, leadership training, and some wise counsel from leaders and friends at the church, I stepped into an open campus administrator role. This was what I had been missing. I was working for the largest, most dynamic church in town. We were seeing more than four thousand people come through our doors every weekend. Just when I thought it couldn't get any better, eLife decided to launch a church back in my hometown of Abernathy and offered me the opportunity to lead that charge. It was a dream I didn't even know I had come true. An opportunity to reach a community where two-thirds would be considered lost with the good news of Jesus.

On our launch weekend, we were immediately the largest church in town with about four hundred attendees. In the first year we saw fifty people begin to follow Jesus, and we had a solid core team who was sold out for Jesus and our church. It was incredible. If the story ended there, it would be a good one, huh?

A little over a year into leading this thriving campus, our Leadership Team heard from the Lord. Scary, right?! Everything our church was and the vision we had was about to change. The Leadership Team introduced me to a Disciple Making Movement strategy that was being used in countries all over the world to reach millions of people. But there was a catch. It would change the way we did church. Instead of being this hip, attractional church, we would look more like the early church, focusing on disciple-making principles, testimony sharing, uncomfortable amounts of prayer, and short trainings on Sundays instead of long sermons. We were making the switch from a knowledge-based church to an obedience-based church.

Can I be honest? I hated every part of the idea. As our pastor began casting the vision to our staff of using this strategy to reach one million people in our West Texas region, I thought, *This dude has fallen off his rocker.* It went against everything I knew that a successful American church should be. I wanted to give up. I wanted to quit. I wanted to find another church to work for.

However, it was in an intense encounter with the Lord that he said, *How are you going to give up on something before you even try it?* I heard him say, *Do you not think I can reach a million people in West Texas?* In the midst of many people leaving our church, challenges at every turn, and persecution, God began reminding me of some things in Scripture. When we follow Jesus, sometimes it leads to persecution. Sometimes it's messy. Sometimes it isn't easy. But obedience is the key.

In the first ten years of eLife, we saw over thirteen thousand people begin to follow Jesus, but it wasn't until I began practicing some of the principles of DMM that God radically began to change my heart. You see, I had always been content with people going to hell. I was content with the few people coming to church whom I had invited, and maybe they would begin following Jesus. For the first time in my life, my heart was burdened for *all* of the one million people in my region who were destined for hell, most of whom would never step into a church. I couldn't bear the thought of missing out on a movement of God because I was unwilling to count the costs of being obedient to Jesus.

So I began regularly joining friends to pray upward of nine to ten hours a week for God to move. I began joining with friends each week, strategically going out among the lost to the "hard" parts of town. It was in those moments that I began to meet and form relationships with people whom I never would have met in my church. It was in those hours of extraordinary prayer that I begin to see God move and answer prayers in ways I never had seen before. It changed my life and what following Jesus looked like for me.

Is it easy? No. Are there difficult and messy days? Absolutely. Is it worth it to see God reach a million people in my region and beyond? There is no doubt in my mind.

In those hard times I think of the faces of Julie, Amy, and others I've met and have seen God begin to move in their lives. It is then when I step back and say yes, it's worth it!

⊶

Chapter 36

Shayne

While I'm telling stories from small West Texas towns, I want you to hear another powerful one. Shayne is the Campus Pastor of our Plains, Texas campus. You might have to locate Plains on a map. I live only an hour away, and when I first heard this town mentioned, even I wasn't sure where it was. Even though it may be a town you haven't heard of, I pray you'll hear of it again someday as a place that was part of catalyzing a movement of God that broke out in West Texas. Shayne leads a group of fired-up people in Plains, and that campus's journey into DMM is one that will inspire you. I'll let Shayne tell the story in his own words.

---∞∞∞---

The story of the Plains campus really began in 2011. Plains is a small town in rural West Texas of about 1,500 people. My wife and I were long-time members of First Baptist Church in Plains, and our pastor and my mentor had just passed away. Before his passing I had been praying and talking with him. I really felt God was leading me into ministry, but I wasn't sure exactly what I was supposed to do. His exact words to me were, "It may not be here," speaking of First Baptist.

After his passing, my wife and I felt a need to start searching with our family for a church. We tried different churches in the area until we tried one church called Experience Life. We loved what was going on and the great welcome we received, but it was an hour away. We told some of our friends about it, and they told us three other families in town had visited as well and that they were thinking and talking about getting the videos and starting a get-together in the old courthouse in Plains. So I contacted them. The two families already had plans to meet the following Sunday. Experience Life was happy to provide them the video and help them get started.

This was the birth of a church that started in Plains called Alive Church. We started meeting every Sunday evening. No pastor, just four families and a video provided by eLife with support from the Executive Pastors. It was amazing. Our numbers started growing on the second week, and we didn't have enough room in the courthouse. My wife and I had just purchased a property in Plains that had a barn, and we had planned on building a house on that land. God had other plans. We agreed to meet in the barn temporarily just to see how things went. We just kept growing. Four families turned into about sixty to seventy people each weekend.

We moved to Sunday mornings after about six months, and things really took off. We still had no pastor, and we were basically just trying to copy whatever eLife was doing. We knew they had a model that was working, so we just copied everything we possibly could to make it feel just the same.

The beauty of it is that we all had roles to play. Our core team and leaders jumped in and greeted, recruited volunteers, and cleaned the facility. You name it, we all did it. As I look back now, I really see that our small church was so successful because we all took ownership and did whatever we had to do to get it done. No matter what!

In some ways I wish I could say that this is the way we stayed and that everything was perfect, but my traditions and others' traditions started to creep in. We wanted a pastor and reached out to the eLife leadership to see if they could help us. They really didn't have any suggestions but did know of one guy we could call and check on. He was from Lubbock, which was an hour away, but we met with him and decided he would be our pastor moving forward. Looking back, we lost a lot of momentum when we did this, because once we hired him and put him in that position, it seems we all stopped doing our part. I really might even need to apologize to him because we expected him to do it all. Isn't that what a pastor is for? Ouch!

Needless to say, we didn't last long with

him. It wasn't his fault. It was ours. Once he was gone we all had to do our part again, and guess what? We started to grow again. We added a band and worship leader who did an awesome job. We kept improving and growing, until once again we thought we really needed a pastor. One of our other leaders and I met with the eLife Executive Pastors again in a restaurant in Lubbock and begged for their help in finding a pastor and becoming an eLife campus. I will never forget that day as one of them looked at me and said, "Guys, a pastor from here is not going to work for you. You need someone local. Have you guys stopped to think that maybe it is one of you who needs to be the pastor?" We both looked at each other, shaking our heads that it couldn't be us.

We left, promising the eLife leaders that we would look local and at least pray about it. My friend and I had a long talk on our way back to Plains, and I told him that I was going to pray about it and really give God a chance to let me know if I might need to consider being the pastor.

I prayed that evening and got in the Word; and it seemed that everything in me was saying, *This is what God has for you.* I gave it a couple more days, and it was something I could not let go of. I asked my wife, and she said that she was behind me in whatever I wanted to do. I called my friend, who was one of the other leaders, and said, "I think I am supposed to do this." We got back in touch with the eLife leadership, and I decided to start pastoring. I was going to try to transition out of my full-time job within the next year. They decided to have me participate in a leadership training program called Protégé. I spent one year in Protégé transitioning to this new position.

In 2016, I became an eLife Campus Pastor, and the Plains church launched as an official eLife campus. We had 168 people on our launch weekend. That will be a day I will never forget. We had a great first year and really made a difference in our community.

It was also in this same year that eLife had their ten-year anniversary. That service was amazing as Chris shared with us the new vision. We also launched over fifty church planters in that service. How awesome is that? We started learning about leveraging everything we had to reach the million. This meant everything we knew and had been doing might change.

I won't lie, I was worried. I had just gotten comfortable with what we were doing, and now I was being asked to give up everything I knew and was comfortable doing. Even as I say that, I realize that if we are comfortable, we are probably not leveraging all that we have for God and his Kingdom.

It was hard. We started focusing more on prayer and the power of the Holy Spirit. Places I have to say I was very weak. Yes, I prayed but not like what we were being challenged to do. Also, I was still "Baptist" at heart and wasn't really sure about the power of the Holy Spirit—ha-ha! I thought only Pentecostals talked about that!

Our services really started to change, and we started challenging our people to get more involved. Not to just come to church and listen or be entertained but to actually listen to God and obey what his Word said. We even started asking people to respond in obedience imme-diately, before they even left the service that day. Our services started turning into some of the most powerful we had ever had! Even though they were powerful, we started noticing people leaving. As I look back today, I realize if God had not grown me, I probably could have been one of those who left because I wasn't comfortable and entertained by what we were doing.

To me, it was a pruning process of starting all over and really making a difference. I agree with Chris that what we were doing in the first ten years was not bad. But eventually we realized that for God to use us to start a movement and reach millions, it requires us to rely completely on him and think outside of the box. We have to do what God says to do!

This is what I felt God calling me to do in Plains. So I talked with the eLife leadership and said, "Guys, I want to lead something different out here. I don't want to have the same service we've been having. I want to lead our group to go all in with DMM and start doing the training on the weekends."

The eLife leadership told me to go for it, and that is exactly what we are doing today. We are doing a lesson per month, really taking it slow so we can obey what God is teaching us in each lesson. It has been very powerful! It is as if we are all doing our part again.

The most important thing is not how many people are sitting in our weekend services anymore. Thank you, God, for helping me see this! One of our members said last week, "I know we don't have as many people coming as we used to, but I feel like we are making more of an impact now for God's Kingdom and making more disciples now than when we had many more people."

We have seen ups and downs in transitioning to DMM in Plains. God is growing us! I'm sure we will struggle more, but that doesn't matter as long as we keep striving to make the biggest impact we can!

⎯⎯⎯ ∞ ⎯⎯⎯

Chapter 37

DMM Push Week

Recently, eLife's Executive Pastor, John, had an idea that was inspired by some of our friends in Africa who have seen a miraculous movement of God break out in their country. John had learned from our African friends that sometimes DMM teams overseas will have seasons where they greatly increase their disciple-making efforts in a short period of time to try to generate some momentum. He wanted to try the same thing.

John wanted to have the eLife staff devote a whole week to prayer, fasting, going out among the lost looking for per-

> *DMM teams overseas will have seasons where they greatly increase their disciple-making efforts in a short period of time to try to generate some momentum.*

sons of peace, and seeing groups started. He suggested that we call it a DMM Push Week. Our Leadership Team loved the idea. We looked for a week within the following few months that had the fewest conflicts, and we officially scheduled the DMM push. We encouraged our staff DMM teams to clear their calendars for that week and asked them to begin praying that God would do something miraculous.

When that week arrived, we were all eager to see what God would do. We had four staff DMM teams that were participating. Each team had between five to ten people on it.

Our teams started with prayer and fasting. We prayed together for two hours on Sunday night and then for another four hours on Monday before going out. We also fasted together as a staff all day Monday, prayed together for another hour each day from 1 to 2 p.m., and then had a testimony time on Friday from 1 to 2 p.m. to tell stories of what God did.

In addition to prayer and fasting, on Tuesday through Friday we went out among the lost for at least two hours each day. Every team went to a different area of town where we had already been working in previous weeks and mapped out a plan to blitz the area over the four days.

My team went back to the neighborhood I referred to in chapter 29 where Billy lived. One of my team members drew a map of the area, divided us into smaller teams of twos and threes, and then sent us to various locations on that map. We hoped to be able to make it to every place on his map by Friday.

I was teamed up with Phil, the finance director on staff at eLife. We went to the first apartment complex assigned to us and began to engage people in spiritual conversations. We were able to talk to people who were standing around outside of their apartments, and we also knocked on doors to see if people were home. We'd usually start the conversation by saying, "We've been praying for this area and wanted to stop by and see if there was any specific way we could pray for you and your family." Most people responded positively to that, and we were able to pray for many people. Depending on how they responded to prayer, we'd look for the opportunity to ask people if they'd be interested in inviting their family members and friends to a Discovery Group where we'd help them discover more about God and his plan for their lives.

In one of the apartment complexes we visited, we met a woman named Kasey. We had knocked on her door; and when she answered, I introduced Phil and myself and then asked our usual question.

Kasey seemed excited we were there and then said to us, "You're never going to believe this." That got our attention. She said that she was talking to her mom just the day before about how she felt that they needed to "grow closer to God." She said she went to her room later that afternoon and said a prayer. She told us that she prayed, *God, if you're real, and if you care about my family, would you send me a sign that you're real and that you care?* After telling us about her prayer, she pointed at us and said, "You are that sign."

I was speechless. She had literally been waiting for us. She asked for a sign from God, and he sent us to her front door the very next morning to offer to pray for her. You can imagine how the rest of the conversation went. She was eager for prayer and had us pray over some needs in her family. Then when we asked her about bringing her friends and family together for a DG, she immediately said she'd love that. In fact, she started telling us who all she'd bring. She said she wanted her mom to come. Then she pointed to a guy walking down the street and said she was going to have him come. She told us about a friend nearby whom she wanted to invite. We saw an oikos opening right before our eyes. We planned to start the DG the following week.

When we left Kasey's apartment that day, I praised God for her responsiveness, but I felt a strong conviction from the Holy Spirit along the lines of Matthew 9:37–38: "Then he

[Jesus] said to his disciples, 'The harvest is plentiful but the workers are few. Ask the Lord of the harvest, therefore, to send out workers into his harvest field.' "

People all over the world just like Kasey are the *plentiful harvest* Jesus talks about in these verses. They are ready to be harvested. They are spiritually open. They would be excited to receive the gospel if someone presented it to them. They are, in a sense, *waiting* for us. They're *waiting* for workers to come and tell them.

According to Jesus, there's just one problem. And I was overwhelmed by the problem that day. Jesus said that the workers are few. There are not many people who are willing to *go* and tell them. In other words, there are many people like Kasey but very few workers like us. Just as Jesus said.

People like Kasey are waiting for us.

How had I missed this all of my life? I assumed that I was a "worker" like Jesus talked about by starting a church, hiring a staff, buying a church building, preaching sermons each weekend, and hoping people like Kasey would *come*. But she didn't come. Neither did most of the harvest. Why would they? Jesus said that workers are supposed to *go* into the harvest fields, not just expect the harvest fields to come to them. His workers were supposed to be *goers*.

Can I be honest? I felt more like a worker in Jesus' harvest that day than I ever had in my entire life. And I was overwhelmed by the fact that the workers in the harvest are still "few," according to Jesus. Lots of people are ready to work if the harvest comes to them, but not many people are *going* into the "plentiful harvest" to work. That has to change if we want to see millions of people touched by God.

As Phil and I continued to work in the harvest that week, we ended up at another door in another apartment complex where someone else was *waiting* for us. Her name was Diane. She

> *Lots of people are ready to work if the harvest comes to them, but not many people are going into the "plentiful harvest" to work.*

happened to be outside her apartment when we arrived, and we asked her if we could pray for her. She was moved by our offer, and when we finished praying for her, she began to wipe the tears from her eyes. We asked her about starting a DG in her apartment complex and she loved the idea. She said that many people in that area need Jesus and that she'd be open to hosting a group in her home. We encouraged her to invite her friends, family, neighbors, and anyone else she could think of. As we talked about this, she said that she wanted to invite her whole apartment complex to come. We were shocked. Most people we talk to aren't that bold. In fact, she said she was going to print out flyers and pass them out to all of her neighbors so that the entire complex could discover more about God together. We couldn't help but begin to ask ourselves, *Could this be our person of peace?* She was already *welcoming* and beginning to *open her oikos* (from the WOOLY acronym in chapter 14). The only thing that remained was watching to see if the open oikos that became a DG would *listen and obey* together. At the time of this writing, the first DG is meeting next week. We can't wait to see what happens.

Phil and I had tons of spiritual conversations during that week. We invited many people to do DGs, and we saw several groups started. I think I can speak for Phil and myself in saying that it was one of the best and most fruitful weeks of our lives. As we began to hear stories from the other teams, we realized we weren't the only ones who were feeling this way. All of the teams were seeing remarkable things happen.

In those 4 days alone, our 4 teams were able to have 424 spiritual conversations, extend 121 DG invitations, and start 29 new groups. In just *one* week!

For context, in the largest years of eLife's first decade, we'd have between one hundred and two hundred first-time guests on an average weekend. In one week of only four teams going out among the lost, there was approximately two to four times the impact—one hundred to two hundred first-time guests compared to more than four hundred spiritual conversations. And it seems obvious that for the average person, the impact of a spiritual conversation would even be greater than just anonymously attending a worship service. Imagine if we had thirty teams out among the lost each week, or fifty teams, or one hundred teams. And imagine if they had regular DMM Push Weeks where they doubled or tripled their efforts. We began to see clearly how the million could truly be reached in ten years. We were so encouraged by what happened that we decided to double our DMM activity every week from that point forward. We also decided to schedule even more DMM Push Weeks in the future.

The current American traditional church model just can't keep up with the impact that could result from many Spirit-empowered ordinary believers going out among the lost to make disciples.

Chapter 38

How to Get Started (Church Staff)

I 'm sure at this point you're wondering, *Okay. This all sounds good, but where do I start?*

In this chapter I will address those who are on an American church staff. In the next chapter I will address those who aren't.

To those of you who are on an American church staff: You have a great opportunity. Chances are, you have many people sitting in your congregation on Sunday mornings who can be mobilized to take part in this with you.

"Cast Vision" and "Train Believers" are two of the 7 Ongoing Elements in a Movement, and you have a built-in audience to whom you can cast vision and train. That means you could begin immediately with multiple DMM church planting teams, as we were able to do at eLife.

If you recall, because we had cast vision and had started training people, by the time we hit our ten-year anniversary, we had already trained more than fifty church planters who were ready to be sent out to form teams and begin to execute the DMM strategy. The next year we were able to cast vision again, sign up more than one hundred people for training, and send out more teams. It's a distinct advantage for sure.

Here are the steps we took at eLife, and I'd recommend them to you also.

Step 1

Senior Pastors, take your entire Leadership Team through a process of exposing them to DMM, getting their buy-in, and forming your WIGTake question.

This is important. The rollout to the church won't go well if the Leadership Team isn't behind it. As a Leadership Team we took three months to read books and discuss DMM before even introducing the concept to our staff or anyone else in our church.

In months 1–3, I asked the Leadership Team to read some of the following books, then we'd discuss them. I'd suggest taking five months and going through all of these in this order:

1. *The Great Evangelical Recession*[1]
2. *Miraculous Movements*[2]
3. *Spent Matches*[3]
4. *Church Planting Movements*[4]
5. *The Kingdom Unleashed*[5]

In addition to these books, I also exposed our Leadership Team to other various DMM resources. You can get a list of these on the Resources page of our blog. I'd encourage you to take them through all of the recommended videos as well.[6]

At the end of these three months, there was 100 percent buy-in from our Leadership Team that DMM was the direction the Lord was leading us in our second decade. After getting the buy-in, we began to work through the WIGTake process, which you can read more about in chapters 1, 2, and 3.

After much discussion, we decided that our WIGTake question was, *What's it going to take to reach 1,000,000 in 10 years so we're on track to reach 200 million in 20 years?* As you recall, we started calling this our "1,000,000 in 10 years vision."

Before finalizing our vision, I went around the room and asked everyone what he or she thought. Everyone agreed this was the vision the Lord wanted us to pursue. Our Leadership Team was united. And that's very important!

At that point, we began to take the Leadership Team through the DMM training, which further solidified the vision.

Note: If you haven't been through DMM training yourself, you need to find a DMM coach who can take you personally through it. Only then will you be ready to take your team through the training. The Executive Team at eLife and I (the ones who oversee the Leadership Team) had gone through the DMM training with a coach long before we started this process with our Leadership Team. The preliminary step of having a DMM coach and going through the training yourself really needs to be completed before you start Step 1. If you don't have a DMM coach already, please contact us, and we'll take you through the training ourselves or help you find a good coach.[7]

Step 2

Roll out the past three months' worth of learning and discovery that you went through with the Leadership Team to the rest of the staff.

Looking back, I could've done better here. I had walked the

Leadership Team through a three-month process, but the staff had to digest the same information in a matter of days. During the staff rollout, I called a meeting where I shared the vision with the staff, and then I sent out a written copy of the vision. I tried to answer as many questions as I could and give as much information as I could with weekly staff updates, but I think there was still quite a bit of confusion initially. In hindsight, I definitely would have extended the initial rollout to our staff.

Another thing I would've done is to take the staff through the DMM training early on. We didn't go through the DMM training as a staff until about a year later, which was a mistake.

Without question, I could've better shepherded the staff through this transition. I feel that I shepherded the Leadership Team well, but not the rest of the staff. Learn from my mistake, and be sensitive to your staff as they try to understand and come along.

Step 3

Begin to brainstorm with your staff to identify the people in your church who you think would be interested in being a part of this. Then meet with these people individually, or in smaller groups, and cast vision to them.

We initially cast vision to a few hundred people, and we had just short of one hundred catch the vision and agree to go through the DMM training.

By the end of the twelve-week DMM training, we had more than fifty people who wanted to move forward and form DMM church planting teams.

Step 4

Develop a plan to roll out the vision to the church.

Since the transition to DMM is a major change for the church, you need to drip the vision to them slowly, rather than all at once. While we couldn't take everyone in the church through the same extensive process we took our Leadership Team, we knew we could develop several sermon series to begin casting the vision. And that's what we did.

We knew we were going to make the big announcement at our ten-year anniversary celebration. This was about a year after we initiated step 1 and several years after our Executive Team and I started processing a transition to DMM. From the time I started praying about DMM with the eLife Executive Team until our church announcement was around three years. Hopefully, that gives you an idea of how extensively we prepared. This is something you want to take your time rolling out in order to gain as much buy-in as possible.

I'd strongly encourage you to do a sermon series at your church, at least a year out from the big announcement, where you talk about the problem. It's important to cast a compelling vision for the problem for people to agree that there's a need for a new solution.

The first series we used to drip the vision to the church was called "Meltdown."[8] This was a series based on the book *The Great Evangelical Recession*. Just as with our Leadership Team, we needed to start the series talking about the problem. Why would we make a major change like this one? Is something wrong? We needed to address the problems in the American church to justify coming up with a different solution from the one we were already implementing.

We had a lot of feedback from that series—both positive and negative. Many people were heartbroken by the trends and statistics in the American church and were eager to do something about it. Others were upset, and probably defensive, of the American church and either didn't want to believe the trends were accurate or didn't want to face them. At that point some decided to go ahead and leave eLife. As I've said in previous chapters, when the model of church you grew up with is critiqued, it can create a variety of responses from different people. Some people can even feel attacked personally because their identity is tied up in a certain way of doing church.

We gave people several months to process what we talked about in that series before revisiting it. About five months later we did another sermon series, but this time it was about the solution to the problem. We called it "Miraculous Movements" and used the book by that same title to share about movements of God breaking out all across the world.[9] We presented these movements as the solution to the problem in the "Meltdown" series. We told powerful stories from Africa and other parts of the world where the trends are positive and the gospel is advancing rapidly.

Three months later, we reached the ten-year anniversary, and it was time to make the big announcement. By that time, thanks to the two sermon series we had completed, I believed our church was ready for the announcement.

Step 5
Announce the transition to the church.

Because we were celebrating our ten-year anniversary, we wanted it to be a big celebration. We rented out the Lubbock Municipal Coliseum and had everyone from our campuses together for one service. Thousands of people came, and we celebrated all that God had done in our first ten years; then we cast vision for what we thought he was leading us to do in our next ten years.

One strategic thing we did—which I would highly recommend to you—was that we commissioned our first DMM Church Planters at this celebration. We had done Step 3 about nine months before our anniversary, so we had DMM Church Planters already trained and ready to go by the time we made the big announcement. At the end of the service, after casting the vision, we had all of the DMM Church Planters come to the front where we laid hands on them and prayed for them as we sent them out from our church to make disciples and plant many more churches.

Step 6

Begin conversations with your staff about how to leverage everything in the church to help with this new vision.

At this point, you've already rolled out the vision to the church, and now you need to begin to leverage every ministry in the church to help with this vision. We were constantly asking the question, "How can we leverage _____ to help us make a million disciples in ten years?" We asked that question about everything we did. Everything was up for discussion.

Step 7

Continue to cast vision, train more people, and share stories of what God is doing.

The hope is that over time many more people in your church will want to become involved. Chances are, the "early adopters" are already involved, but there are some people who want to learn more, give it time, hear the stories, and process all of it before buying in. That's okay. Give them time. Don't pressure them. Keep the DMM vision at the forefront and continue to offer opportunities for people to be trained.

Step 8

Meet with your DMM coach regularly to keep "raising the sails" and preparing for movement.

I can't stress enough how important coaching is. We wouldn't be where we are without our DMM coach. Be sure to meet with your coach regularly, and let him or her continue to guide you through next steps.

God brings a movement. Our job is to raise the sails and pray our hearts out.

Remember that only God brings a movement. Our job is to raise the sails and pray our hearts out. Keep doing that until movement comes or the Lord takes you home!

Chapter 39

How to Get Started (Church Attendees)

F or those of you who aren't on an American church staff,
how should you get started?

I mentioned that the folks on an American church staff
have a great opportunity in starting DMM because they
already have people to whom they can cast vision and train.
You also have a great opportunity in that you don't have the
day-to-day and weeknight ministry responsibilities that a
person on a church staff has. That means you may have more
time than they do to "go out among the lost" and see groups
started. That's a distinct advantage too.

Here are the steps I'd recommend to you.

Step 1

Cast vision to some of your fired-up friends and family to go
through a DMM training with you.

It's always best to go through training with people whom
you could see being on your future DMM church planting
team. Once you find two or three friends to go through training with you, approach a DMM coach anywhere in the nation
(or around the world) to do a DMM training with you via

the videoconferencing platform of your choice. This is how my team and I were trained because our DMM coach lived overseas in Dubai. Again, if you don't know of a DMM coach already, please contact us, and we'll take you through the training ourselves or help you find a good DMM coach.[1]

In addition to the training, consider reading some of the books I mentioned in my recommendations to American church staffs. This will speed up your exposure to DMM and what God is doing around the world.

Step 2

Once you've been through the training, talk to the people who trained with you about whether or not they want to move forward and form a DMM church planting team. Once you figure out who's excited to move forward, formalize the team and begin to meet weekly under the direction of your DMM coach.

Step 3

Start "raising the sails" for movement by putting into practice the 7 Ongoing Elements of a Movement that you learned about in your DMM training.

1. Focus on God's Word
2. Multiply Extraordinary Prayer
3. Go Out Among the Lost
4. See Groups Start
5. Cast Vision
6. Train Believers
7. Ongoing Coaching

Keep your team accountable in doing these things when you meet together each week. As you begin to put these into practice, it won't be long before you'll have powerful stories to tell from going out among the lost and seeing groups start.

Step 4

If you're currently attending an American church, begin to cast vision for what you're doing to the church staff.

One of the best ways to cast vision for DMM to American church pastors is exposure. They need to hear what God is doing all over the world. Buy them the books I've recommended. Consider sharing some of our blog posts with them. Share the videos and other resources with them that are on the Resources page of our blog.[2] It will be difficult for them to get excited about seeing this implemented in the church they lead without exposure to how God is using movements to reach millions all over the world. Exposure is the key.

Also, pray for your pastor and the church staff that God would open their hearts to what they read and the videos they watch. Pray that God would give them a hunger to see millions of disciples made and churches planted and not to be satisfied with the American church model. Many pastors will admit that the American church is struggling and is not getting the job done. They're just not always sure what needs to change.

Tell your pastor and the church staff the stories of what God is doing through you and your team. Tell them about the people you've met, the groups you've started, and the fruit you've borne. Stories are powerful!

If the staff begins to catch the vision, offer to take them through the DMM training so they can learn more, or offer to connect them with your DMM coach who could take them through the training.

Let me say this, though. If the pastors and staff don't catch the vision, don't be discouraged. They don't have to catch it in order for *you* to be a part of a movement. Sure, it could be helpful to have your church's backing because they have so many people who could be trained easily and sent, but movements are breaking out all over the world in places with no existing churches. So don't be discouraged if your church doesn't get on board.

Your continuing to raise the sails, even if your church doesn't want to participate, shouldn't threaten your church leadership or staff at all. Movements are about reaching lost people, and those people don't go to your church. What you're doing won't likely interfere with what your church is doing at all.

Step 5

Meet with your DMM coach regularly to keep "raising the sails" and preparing for movement. This is the same last step I used in the last chapter for American church staff members.

Always stay close to your coach, and remember that our responsibility is to raise the sails—God brings movement. Keep raising those sails and praying your heart out that God would bring a movement to your region! Perhaps God will answer those prayers, and perhaps you'll get to be right in the middle of it!

Perhaps God will answer those prayers for movement, and perhaps you'll get to be right in the middle of it!

Chapter 40

Can This Really Happen in America?

I've asked this same question before. Usually it comes out of the mouth of someone who's skeptical about the viability of movements in America. And, of course, I've been there. Typically, the objections go something like this:

> The culture is different in America than in Africa
> and Asia where some of these movements have
> broken out. I'm not sure if our culture is well
> suited for movements.
>   We are an individualistic culture. African
> and Asian cultures are more communal. It makes
> sense that movements would take hold there
> because people make decisions in groups, but we
> don't in America. We're not influenced as easily
> by our close friends and family, which means a
> movement would be less likely to happen here.

Add ecclesiological concerns to the list, and things get more worrisome.

America is dominated by churches with buildings, money, and pastors who want to keep their jobs and, therefore, are motivated to keep people in pews. Wouldn't the traditional American church fight movements for these reasons, making movements less likely to occur? The clergy/laity divide in America is strong and likely hard to overcome. In movements, you need the laity to act like the clergy, and that might not be well received in our country, as the clergy can be possessive of their roles.

Oh, and what about educational concerns?

We're a more educated country than many of the countries where movements have broken out. Since movements rely so heavily on signs and wonders, many in our country don't even believe in those because proof-based logic rules rather than faith. Can a movement really thrive where science rules the day and miracles are largely written off?

I've raised the objections too. I've asked these same questions. When I asked Stan, "Can this really happen in America?" his response was perfect. He replied, "Movements typically break out in all of the places where people said there's no way it could happen there."

And he was right. People said there was no way it could happen in China. Then it happened in China. People said there was no way it could happen in India. Then it happened in India. People said there was no way it could happen in Africa. Then it happened in Africa. People said there was no way it could happen in the Middle East. Then it happened in the Middle East.

Doesn't that sound like God? He loves doing the things that we consider impossible. "This

> "Movements typically break out in all of the places where people said there's no way it could happen there." –Stan Parks

foolish plan of God is wiser than the wisest of human plans, and God's weakness is stronger than the greatest of human strength" (1 Corinthians 1:25).

If you're questioning whether America is ready, find reassurance in the fact that so many people say it could never happen here. That makes America one of the most likely places for a movement to break out next.

In a particular part of India, missionary after missionary, for generations, went there and saw very little fruit. The ground was hard. The people were unresponsive. Guess what people were saying? There's no way a movement could happen there. I'm sure they had their list of reasons just as we have ours.

Well, guess what? One of the greatest movements of God in history has broken out in that area in the last twenty to thirty years. Millions have been baptized.

I guess the naysayers got it wrong again.

So, can this happen in America? The real answer is, it already is happening in America!

In recent years, through a nonprofit organization called Cityteam,[1] a movement has been sparked in California. Our team flew there last year to witness it for ourselves, and it's truly remarkable.

So, can this happen in America? The real answer is, it already is happening in America!

I emailed Hermie, a movements catalyst on staff at Cityteam, to ask for an update. In the last six years, Cityteam has seen more than 120,000 disciples made and more than 11,000 groups and churches started. This movement started in America, but it didn't end up only in America. It has spread to quite a few other countries as people who became disciples here moved back to their home countries and made disciples there. Most of the other countries impacted by this movement are in the Caribbean and Central America.

Hermie said,

> What sets these replicating disciples apart from regular believers is the ecosystem we are intentional at creating for them to germinate, develop a root system, receive water and nutrients to grow and bear fruit resulting in transformation and more disciples that do the same.
>
> That ecosystem is the Kingdom of God that has come to their personal life, their home, their work and their neighborhood. To do this, our disciple-making teams are intentional at helping, modeling and setting expectations for those they disciple to:
>
> 1. Read the Bible regularly (daily if possible)
> 2. Not just learn the content, but apply what they learn
> 3. Share those lessons on their spiritual journey with others
> 4. This is done in community with other family members

and/or friends who hold each other accountable to apply and share

5. They love and serve one another in practical ways
6. They actively pursue loving and serving their neighbors in practical ways also
7. With the goal to replicate this ecosystem by starting another group that starts more groups[2]

We witnessed this firsthand. We heard the stories. We went to the neighborhoods where this had broken out. It's remarkable!

We even saw the very long diagram depicting the generations of this movement in their office. In some countries it's in the first or second generation. In other countries it's in the third, fourth, or fifth generation. And in one country it has even reached the tenth generation!

We don't have to ask whether this can happen in America. This *is* happening in America. The question is, will we join God in what he is already doing in our country?

Cityteam is not the only successful DMM practitioner in America. A movement researcher has gathered data indicating that movements are happening in two or even three places in our country. And researchers are currently tracking more than thirty places in the United States where they are seeing second- and third-generation churches. Many of these could cross the fourth-generation threshold to become sustained movements at some point in the future. You just don't hear these stories told as often—DMM is still more underground at this point.

> *The question is, will we join God in what he is already doing in our country?*

Wouldn't you love for a movement to break out in your region? Perhaps God wants to bring a movement to your region, but he's waiting on courageous men and women to raise the sails.

Will you raise the sails? Will you do whatever it takes to see everyone in your region and, ultimately, in your people group reached?

Will you raise the sails? Will you do whatever it takes to see everyone in your region and, ultimately, in your people group reached?

Roy Moran, one of my DMM coaches, and author of *Spent Matches*, wrote,

> How much do we love the mission that Jesus gave us? Is it worth the sacrifice of our lives to stop the trends we are experiencing today? Are we willing to expose our inflexible misread of the Bible and rethink our methods? Would we be willing to keep asking the question, "What needs to be done?" and not default to the cop-out, "I'll just do what I can do"?[3]

Pastors and leaders, will you and your church join us in "raising the sails"? I know of only one other church in America that is trying to raise DMM sails for movement. It's the church where Roy Moran is pastor. There may be others, but it's the only one I'm familiar with. Most of the places in America where movement activity is being seen are not through traditional American churches.

I read a quote years ago in David Garrison's book *Church Planting Movements*, and I have read it to our staff over and over again. It describes our biggest struggle with regard to these movements. Garrison says,

> If you are going to see a Church Planting Movement, you're going to have to make some room for it. One of the toughest things for good people to do is to give up the many good things they are already doing in order to embrace the best. Perhaps this describes you. You are excited about a new vision of possibilities but hate the thought of leaving behind the many good things you are already doing. But if what you are doing now hasn't led you to a Church Planting Movement, then perhaps it is time for a change. If you keep doing what you've been doing, you'll keep getting what you've been getting. So, if you're not already seeing a Church Planting Movement with what you're doing now, you should stop, clear some space, and try something new. Remember, a good definition of insanity is to keep doing what you've been doing, while expecting different results.[4]

Pastors and leaders, we've got to make some room for a Church Planting Movement. Clearly, what we've been doing hasn't led to CPM in our country. Isn't it time for a change? Let's heed these words of wisdom and "stop, clear some space, and try something new"! We have so many people in our churches whom we could mobilize to be a part of this. The more teams we send out, the more people we can reach!

Remember, Jesus said, "The harvest is plentiful but the

workers are few" (Matthew 9:37 NIV). The problem isn't with the harvest. The problem isn't with our people group. There are many in our people group who are prepared to become disciples of Jesus who make disciples. The problem is that the workers are few! There aren't many people going to the lost. That's definitely true in DMM. There are hardly any workers.

Typically, in America, if people won't come to our churches, they won't be reached. We spend most of our week planning a big Sunday event that we're hoping our city will attend. Look around. They're not coming.

> *We spend most of our week planning a big Sunday event that we're hoping our city will attend. Look around. They're not coming.*

In most places less than 10 percent of the population is evangelical Christian, according to the research done in *The Great Evangelical Recession*.[5] Who is chasing after the other 90 percent? Who is working among the 90 percent who would never darken the doors of an American church? There are 200,000,000 in our people group in America who are in that 90 percent.

For the first ten years we tried to put on as attractive and powerful of a weekend service as we knew how. But what we found is that most of the city didn't come.

Jesus didn't say put on a worship service and invite people to come. Jesus said "*Go* and make disciples of all the nations"! (Matthew 28:19, italics mine). Jesus said *go*, and for the first ten years, I now realize that we *stayed*. If they came, we'd reach them; but if they didn't come, I guess they were out of luck.

You know what's so disheartening? As our team is now going out among the lost in some of the most difficult parts of town, it's apparent than *no one* else is working in these areas.

No one else is *going* to these people. But many of these people are *hungry.* Many of these people will be our persons of peace who will help us reach a whole neighborhood or apartment complex. But the American strategy is not primarily a *go* strategy.

I'm not saying there's anything wrong with a *come* strategy. Clearly, 10 percent might come. But what about the other 90 percent? Who's going to go to them?

Will you be a worker? Will you join us in going to the 90 percent? We can't reach the million on our own. We need other churches and organizations to partner with us in this pursuit. We need many churches, denominations, networks, and organizations sending out disciple makers and church planters to *go* and reach the 90 percent.

> *Will you be a worker? Will you join us in going to the 90 percent?*

After Jesus said that "the harvest is plentiful, but the workers are few," he said, "Ask the Lord of the harvest, therefore, to send out workers into his harvest field" (Matthew 9:38 NIV). What's the solution to the worker shortage? We have to *pray!* That's what our church is doing right now. We're praying for *you!* We're praying that the Lord would send you and your team out as workers into his fields. We're praying that many other American churches would join us on this disciple-making mission. We're praying that many American Christians would get tired of the status quo and, like Paul, would say, "But my life is worth nothing to me unless I use it for finishing the work assigned me by the Lord Jesus—the work of telling others the Good News about the wonderful grace of God" (Acts 20:24).

We have a task to finish. We have a work to complete.

> *Let's raise the sails together! Come, Holy Spirit, and blow on our sails!*

The harvest is ready for us. They are waiting. The workers are few. Hear the Lord of the harvest calling *you* to be a worker in his field!

Let's raise the sails *together*! Come, Holy Spirit, and blow on our sails!

Epilogue: Our Progress

A fter our ten-year anniversary celebration in September
of 2017, the fifty-four church planters whom we commissioned at that service spent the rest of the semester
training their teams. Most of our DMM church planting
teams launched officially at the beginning of 2018. For the
first few months of 2018, these teams spent most of their time
prayer walking their areas of focus to prepare the soil for them
to go out among the lost (see chapter 14) and see groups start
(see chapter 15). I want to share with you some of what God
has done in the eight months since they started.

We have 51 DGs currently that were started by our DMM
church planting teams. Multiple streams of these DGs have
reached second-generation growth, and one stream has even
reached third-generation growth. Three of these DGs have
been started in Thailand through a local partner we trained
in DMM.

We have eighty-five church planters on fourteen DMM
church planting teams who are executing the DMM strategy. The leaders of these teams meet in three different DMM
coaching groups for weekly ongoing coaching.

We've cast vision to and trained 314 church planters since
the spring of 2017, with 215 of those being trained since the

beginning of 2018. While not everyone chooses to move forward at the end of the training, those who do will form teams to begin executing this strategy with us. I anticipate that the 14 DMM church planting teams will grow to 20 to 25 teams by the end of the year. I also anticipate that the number of DGs will double by the end of the year based on current trends.

These DMM church planting teams are tracking the number of hours they're spending in corporate prayer; the number of spiritual conversations they have when they're out among the lost; and the number of DG invitations they extend. In the last year, these teams have accumulated thousands of hours of prayer together; they have had thousands of spiritual conversations; and they have extended many invitations to people to engage in a DG. As a result, we've seen many groups started.

As you can see, we're just beginning; but in a relatively short period of time, we've seen God do miraculous things. We are by no means a "movement" yet, as defined by multiple streams of fourth-generation churches; but as we execute the DMM strategy and raise the sails, we pray that the Holy Spirit would blow on our sails and allow us to be a part of a movement very soon.

The way we leverage each area at our church is still very fluid. We are constantly evaluating all that we're doing, praying about how to leverage it best for movement, and changing accordingly. Our philosophy lately has been that we're willing to try anything. If our Youth Pastor feels led to try something in the Youth Ministry that he or she thinks could better leverage it for movement, we've told them to go for it. If a Campus Pastor feels led to try something on the weekend that he thinks could better leverage it for movement, we've told them to give it a shot. And so forth. With each idea, we'll evaluate it over time, and if it helps us accomplish our mission, we'll keep it. If it proves to be unhelpful or distracting, we'll discard it. Some of what I've shared in this book, like how we're currently leveraging the weekend, could change in the coming days as we learn and grow. We are consistently asking the WIGTake question: *What's it going to take to reach 1,000,000 in 10 years?* We'll continue to keep you updated on our progress at wigtakedmm.com.

If you are interested in taking a team through the DMM training, one of our DMM coaches will gladly lead you through the twelve lessons if you're willing to obey and share whatever the Holy Spirit teaches you, *regardless of the cost.* Reread that last part. If you take this seriously, I'm almost certain you'll have to count a cost.

If you've considered the cost and are still interested, contact us at info@wigtakedmm.com, and we'll let you know when the next training is starting.

One more disclaimer: If you think you've already got it all figured out, this training is probably not for you. But if you're inspired by what God is doing overseas, and you're open to releasing the way American church was done in the twentieth century, this training may be just what you've been looking for.

Questions for Discussion

Chapter 1: What Is WIGTake?
1. What is your biggest takeaway from this chapter?
2. Jesus encouraged his disciples to have a vision for reaching two hundred million people. How many people do you have a vision for reaching? Can your current strategy accomplish that vision?
3. How do you think formulating your WIGTake question could help you and your ministry?

Chapter 2: 1,000,000 in 10 Years
1. What is your biggest takeaway from this chapter?
2. How many people are in your people group?
3. Do you have a vision to reach all of them or just a few?
4. If you develop a plan to reach all of them in twenty years and work backward, how many do you need to reach this year? In the next five years? In the next ten years?
5. Taking all of this into consideration, what is your WIGTake?

Chapter 3: The Whiteboard
1. What is your biggest takeaway from this chapter?
2. Can your current strategy accomplish a vision to reach your entire people group? If not, why?

3. How much does it cost you to baptize one person at your church? Is that cost scalable to reaching your people group?
4. What bothered you most about the current trends in the American church?
5. Do you agree with the concept that to restore a culture of discipleship we need to release the way the American church was done in the twentieth century? Why, or why not?

Chapter 4: Millions

1. What is your biggest takeaway from this chapter?
2. What impresses you most about these movements happening around the world?
3. How do you think the movement in India was able to get the cost per baptism down to 66 cents?
4. What do you think keeps most people from believing that a million disciples could be made in ten years when God is already doing much more than that in other parts of the world?
5. What are the differences between the disciple-making strategies in the Gospels and Acts and the disciple-making strategy in your church?
6. Do you sincerely believe that God could use you to reach millions? Why, or why not? Be honest.

Chapter 5: What Is DMM?

1. What is your biggest takeaway from this chapter?
2. After reading the definitions of DMM in this chapter, how would you put the definition into your own words?
3. Why do you think most people treat their "method" of doing church as sacred when it might be uncommon in other parts of the world where believers are seeing movement?

4. How would you explain "generational discipleship" to someone? Why is it so important for movement?
5. The average size of the more than 650 active movements in the world today is 75,000 believers. How do you think movements grow to be so large?
6. Do you think that DMM is a strategy that your church needs to consider, as eLife did? Why, or why not?

Chapter 6: The Ten-Year Anniversary

1. What is your biggest takeaway from this chapter?
2. Why do you think that ordinary people in these movements overseas often refer to themselves as church planters? Why do you believe we do not think of ourselves that way?
3. What stood out to you about the elephants and rabbits illustration?
4. Do you agree with Stan and Jerry that elephant churches can't reach our people group on their own and that they need many rabbit churches to help them? If so, why?

Chapter 7: Leverage

1. What is your biggest takeaway from this chapter?
2. Do you like change, or do you tend to resist change? Why?
3. Why do you think it was important for eLife to reevaluate every ministry and leverage them for DMM?
4. How much time does your church spend on prayer and testimony in the weekend services? Do you think it's enough? If not, why don't you think your church does those things more?
5. At your church, is there more teaching or training? Is the focus on obedience or information transfer?
6. Do you think you'd want to be a part of a weekend gathering

that focused on prayer, testimony, and training? Do you think others would? What would be the concerns?

Chapter 8: Where's Chris?

1. What is your biggest takeaway from this chapter?
2. At your church, does one person do most of the teaching or are there "many" teachers? Why do you think your church does it this way?
3. Why do you think it was important to Paul and Barnabas that "many" were preaching the word of the Lord in Antioch? Why not just Paul?
4. Have you ever found in your own life that you were more excited about the messenger than the message? What are the dangers in this?
5. Why do you think America has a "celebrity preacher" culture? Is this healthy for the church?
6. Why is it so important for all of us to "preach" if we want to see a movement?

Chapter 9: DMM Coaching

1. What is your biggest takeaway from this chapter?
2. Why is coaching so important?
3. Does your pastor have a disciple-making/church planting coach? Do you? Why, or why not?

Chapter 10: DMM Training

1. What is your biggest takeaway from this chapter?
2. Why was it strategic for Stan not to give Chris all of the training sheets at the very beginning? Why do you think he waited?
3. Have you ever been a part of a Bible study where the leader

didn't let the group move on until everyone obeyed the previous lesson? Why do you think most groups don't operate this way? Why do most people move on whether they've obeyed or not?

4. Why do you think Stan primarily asked us questions and pointed us to Scripture rather than teaching us?
5. What's keeping you and a group of your friends from going through a DMM training together? Why not start a training as soon as possible?

Chapter 11: Raise the Sails

1. What is your biggest takeaway from this chapter?
2. Why do you think the sailboat analogy is the one Stan used often with us to describe movements?
3. What is helpful to you personally about that analogy?

Chapter 12: Focus on God's Word

1. What is your biggest takeaway from this chapter?
2. When you read the Bible, is your focus on obeying immediately what you read and sharing it with others? Why, or why not?
3. Do you agree with Roy that many people would give the church today a "low grade" on obedience to Jesus' commands? Why, or why not?
4. Do you measure your own spiritual growth by how much you're *obeying* Jesus and the Bible or how much you *know about* Jesus and the Bible? Why is it important to focus on obedience?
5. Questions 6 and 7 in the DBS process are some of the most important questions to ask when we read God's Word but some of the least often asked. Why do you think that is so, if those questions are key to movement?
6. What stands out to you about the DBS process?

7. What do you need to do or change to better focus on God's Word?

Chapter 13: Multiply Extraordinary Prayer

1. What is your biggest takeaway from this chapter?
2. What stands out to you about the way people pray in these movements overseas?
3. Why do you think "extraordinary prayer" is found in every Church Planting Movement?
4. What is "ordinary" for you right now in your prayer life? What could you add to make it "extraordinary"?
5. What do you need to do or change to better multiply extraordinary prayer?

Chapter 14: Go Out Among the Lost

1. What is your biggest takeaway from this chapter?
2. Why do you think it's so challenging for Christians to "go out among the lost"?
3. Why do you think the "person of peace" principle from Matthew 10 and Luke 10 is so important in movements?
4. A person of peace is WOOLY. Review what each of those letters stands for and talk about some people you know who might be WOOLY.
5. What do you need to do or change to better go out among the lost?

Chapter 15: See Groups Start

1. What is your biggest takeaway from this chapter?
2. Why is it so important to start DGs with lost people?
3. Describe in your own words what four generations of groups would look like.

4. What do you need to do or change to better see groups start?

Chapter 16: Cast Vision

1. What is your biggest takeaway from this chapter?
2. Research from these movements shows that a team of two to three people can reach 100,000. What did you think when you read that?
3. Do you agree that the American church can "suppress the gifts, ambitions, and callings of ordinary believers"? How does this happen?
4. What do you think will be most challenging about casting to ordinary Christians the vision that God wants to use them to make many disciples and plant many churches?
5. What do you need to do or change to better cast vision?

Chapter 17: Train Believers

1. What is your biggest takeaway from this chapter?
2. Why is it so important in the DMM training not to move on to the next lesson until you obey the current lesson?
3. Why do you think that training is such a vital component in movements?
4. What do you need to do or change to better train believers?

Chapter 18: Ongoing Coaching

1. What is your biggest takeaway from this chapter?
2. Why is it important to find a coach who has experienced what you want to experience rather than a coach who is trying to help you experience something he or she has never seen personally?
3. Why should we be looking outside of America for help in seeing movements started here?

4. Why do you think Americans are so unaware of the remarkable things God is doing overseas? And if we hear about them, why do you think we are so slow to reach out to overseas friends for mentoring?

5. What do you need to do or change to better pursue ongoing coaching?

Chapter 19: Akachi

1. What is your biggest takeaway from this chapter?
2. What inspires you about Akachi's life?
3. Do you think God could use you as he used Akachi?

Chapter 20: Andrew and Kristin

1. What is your biggest takeaway from this chapter?
2. What inspires you about Andrew and Kristin's story?
3. How do you think Andrew and Kristin make so much time to "go out among the lost" and "multiply extraordinary prayer" if they have full-time jobs and children?

Chapter 21: From Microsoft to Ministry

1. What is your biggest takeaway from this chapter?
2. When God sets a mom or dad on fire, it can spread to the children. If you have children, are you giving them a great example to follow like Chris's dad gave him? If not, what needs to change?
3. Have you ever had disappointments in your life that you realize now, in hindsight, were a part of God's plan to prepare you for the future? If so, what were they?

Chapter 22: Seminary Elective

1. What is your biggest takeaway from this chapter?

2. Why do you think "church planting" is so uncommon in many towns across America, just as it was in Chris's town?
3. What stands out to you about the simple churches Chris learned about at the church planting conference?
4. Why do you think churches that start out simple can so easily give in to the temptation to become complex, and thus more difficult to reproduce?

Chapter 23: From Simple to Complex

1. What is your biggest takeaway from this chapter?
2. At what point do you think eLife took the turn from simplicity to complexity?
3. Have you ever asked the question, "What would it take for us to see a great movement of God in our country like they're seeing overseas?" Either way, what do you think it's going to take?
4. Does your church have the attitude of, "If we find a strategy that better fulfills the Great Commission than our current strategy, we'll abandon what we've been doing and pursue that strategy"? If not, why?

Chapter 24: Identity Crisis

1. What is your biggest takeaway from this chapter?
2. If you're an American church pastor, have you ever had an identity crisis like the one described in this chapter? If so, explain. If you're not an American church pastor, have you ever had an identity crisis that helps you identify with the ones described in this chapter? If so, explain.
3. Why do you think the transition into DMM for a church can be described as a "death experience"?
4. Why do you think the transition into DMM often results in an

identity crisis? How should those who are transitioning address this?

Chapter 25: A Reduction in Giving

1. What is your biggest takeaway from this chapter?
2. What are some of the reasons it is so important for your church to be conservative financially?
3. Why is debt so dangerous? How can debt drown a church and the vision God might have for it?

Chapter 26: A Reduction in Attendance

1. What is your biggest takeaway from this chapter?
2. Why do so many churches measure success by how many people come and sit in the auditorium during a weekend? Is that the best measure of a church's success?
3. How is it that Jesus preached to thousands while he was here on earth but there were only 120 gathered in an upper room in Acts 1 after he ascended into heaven? Where did everyone go?
4. If a transition into DMM could mean that half your church leaves, would you still have the courage to make the transition if you sensed God leading you to?

Chapter 27: Doubts and Discouragement

1. What is your biggest takeaway from this chapter?
2. What are some of the doubts you have about DMM? Why do you think you've had these?
3. How should a pastor or team handle discouragement, especially as it relates to transitioning to DMM?
4. Why do you think many Christians are more concerned about whether or not their church is doing things they like, rather

than whether or not their elders have heard from the Lord and are doing what God likes?

5. Why do you think many American churches are not primarily "missionary" in nature but more consumeristic? Why are many of our churches designed this way?

6. Why do you think there is opposition for those who decide to transition into DMM, much like what Jerry Trousdale describes at the end of the chapter quoted from *Miraculous Movements*?

Chapter 28: PIPSY

1. What is your biggest takeaway from this chapter?

2. Why is gaining access to the area to which God has led you to go so important?

3. Why do you think "serving people" is the number one way people all over the world who execute a DMM strategy find people who are interested in God?

4. What stands out to you about the PIPSY acronym?

5. Why do you think that non-PIPSY places tend to be less receptive to spiritual conversations and prayer?

Chapter 29: Poor

1. What is your biggest takeaway from this chapter?

2. Why do you think virtually every Church Planting Movement in the world today has been started among the poor?

3. Have you ever asked a stranger if you could pray for him or her? If so, how did the person respond?

4. Why is it so important to ask the DG question as much as possible?

5. Why do you think Christians sometimes don't have great reputations in poorer communities?

6. Can you think of some "poorer" parts of your town where God might be leading you to make disciples?

Chapter 30: International

1. What is your biggest takeaway from this chapter?
2. Have you ever taken part in the Perspectives class? If so, how was your experience? If not, why not sign up today?
3. What do you think impacted Kate and Lucy the most during their exchange years?
4. Have you ever had an international into your home for dinner? If so, how did it go? If you haven't, why?

Chapter 31: Prisoner

1. What is your biggest takeaway from this chapter?
2. Why do you think prisoners are so receptive to the gospel?
3. Have you ever been inside of a prison to share the gospel, pray for people, or lead Bible studies? If so, how would you describe the experience? If not, take some time to pray about getting involved in some way.

Chapter 32: Sick

1. What is your biggest takeaway from this chapter?
2. Have you ever prayed for someone and seen the person healed? If so, share about the experience.
3. God is using miracles in these movements overseas to bring millions to faith in Jesus. Would you be comfortable with God using you to pray for miracles in your context? Why, or why not?
4. Why do you think Jesus told the disciples to "heal the sick" as a part of their strategy for going into a new area?

Chapter 33: Tentmaking

1. What is your biggest takeaway from this chapter?
2. What do you think is the greatest barrier to businesspeople seeing themselves as church planters?
3. If Paul couldn't have planted an "American" model of church because of the time, money, and resources required, why is it our primary strategy to plant these? Why don't we plant more churches like the ones Paul planted that don't require so much time, money, and resources?
4. How important is it for leaders of a DMM strategy to model for people that it's possible to carry a full-time job and still make disciples and plant churches?

Chapter 34: Weekend Planning

1. What is your biggest takeaway from this chapter?
2. Why is it important for us to organize our trainings around the DBS questions?
3. Why do you think we've found that ten- to twelve-minute trainings tend to be more effective week to week than thirty- to thirty-five-minute sermons?
4. Why do you think eLife now has so many people involved in each of their services?

Chapter 35: Ty

1. What is your biggest takeaway from this chapter?
2. Why do you think Ty resisted initially the idea of transitioning to a DMM strategy?
3. How do you think Ty got past his resistance and became one of DMM's greatest proponents?

Chapter 36: Shayne

1. What is your biggest takeaway from this chapter?
2. Why do you think the church in Plains was searching so hard for an official "pastor" when they were doing well leading it themselves?
3. Why do you think Shayne and the other leaders of the Plains campus decided to turn off the eLife messages on the weekends and start doing DMM training with the people who remained?

Chapter 37: DMM Push Week

1. What is your biggest takeaway from this chapter?
2. If the harvest is plentiful, why do you think the workers are still few? Why haven't more workers gone into the harvest?
3. Why is the American church often expecting the lost to come to us rather than our going to them?
4. Do you think a DMM Push Week could be helpful to you and your team? Why, or why not?

Chapter 38: How to Get Started (Church Staff)

1. What is your biggest takeaway from this chapter?
2. What next steps do you need to take to get started?
3. What are the biggest challenges in getting started?
4. Are you willing to spend a season praying about whether God would have you transition your church to DMM and go through the recommended resources? If he speaks to you and encourages you to move forward, will you follow him regardless of the cost?

Chapter 39: How to Get Started (Church Attendees)

1. What is your biggest takeaway from this chapter?
2. What next steps do you need to take to get started?
3. What are the biggest challenges with getting started?
4. Are you willing to spend a season praying about whether God would have you move forward with DMM and go through the recommended resources? If he speaks to you and encourages you to move forward, will you follow him regardless of the cost?

Chapter 40: Can This *Really* Happen in America?

1. What is your biggest takeaway from this chapter?
2. Why do you think so many people question whether or not movements could happen in America? What do you think is the best response to the skepticism?
3. What do you think will be people's greatest challenge in "raising the sails" for movement in their area?
4. David Garrison challenges us that if what we're currently doing hasn't led to a Church Planting Movement, it's time for a change. Has what you're currently doing led to a Church Planting Movement? If not, are you open to changing and trying something new?
5. Why are most churches content with pursuing the 10 percent of people in an area interested in church to the neglect of the 90 percent of people in an area who aren't interested? Why do churches have more of a *come* strategy than a *go* strategy?
6. Are you willing to give up everything you have and do whatever it takes to see a movement break out in your area? Why, or why not?

Appendix 1

Seven-Question DBS Process

1. What are you thankful for in the past week?
2. What has challenged or stressed you or others around you in the past week?
3. Is there anything this group can do to help with those challenges or stresses, or is there any other need we can meet together?

   At this point, read a passage of Scripture several times out loud together; then have everyone in the group retell it in their own words. Ask the next four questions of the group.

4. What does this passage teach you about God?
5. What does the passage teach you about people?
6. What should you do this week in response to the passage?
7. Who should you share with this week?

   In addition to these questions, before you read the new passage for the week, you'll review last week's passage and ask if everyone did what they said they were going to do and shared with whom they said they would. Doing this keeps everyone accountable for *obeying* and *sharing*. See chapter 12 for a more in-depth explanation.

Appendix 2

Creation to Christ Passages

Genesis 1:1–25

Genesis 2:4–24

Genesis 3:1–13

Genesis 3:14–24

Genesis 6:5–8

Genesis 6:9–8:14

Genesis 8:15–9:17

Genesis 12:1–8; 15:1–6; 17:1–7

Genesis 22:1–19

Exodus 12:1–28

Exodus 20:1–21

Leviticus 4:1–35

Isaiah 53

Luke 1:26–38; 2:1–20

Matthew 3; John 1:29–34

Matthew 4:1–11

John 3:1–21

John 4:1–26, 39–42

Luke 5:17–26

Mark 4:35–41

Mark 5:1–20

John 11:1–44

Matthew 26:17–30

John 18:1–19:16

Luke 23:32–56

Luke 24:1–35

Luke 24:36–53

John 3:1–21

Resources

To continue following the DMM journey of Experience Life, visit wigtakedmm.com.

For recommendations of helpful DMM books and videos, visit wigtakedmm.com/resources.

To contact us directly, email us at info@wigtakedmm.com.

Notes

Chapter 1: What Is WIGTake?
[1] Experience Life Church, http://www.experiencelifenow.com.

[2] wigtakedmm.com, http://www.wigtakedmm.com/resources.

[3] David Garrison, *Church Planting Movements: How God Is Redeeming a Lost World* (Midlothian, VA: WIGTake Resources, 2004), 40.

[4] Joshua Project, People Groups; the "Kui Khond" page, https://joshuaproject.net/people_groups/19065.

[5] Garrison, 89.

[6] Garrison, 94.

[7] Garrison, 279.

[8] Wikipedia, "World Population Estimates" entry, last modified September 20, 2018, https://en.wikipedia.org/wiki/World_population_estimates.

Chapter 2: 1,000,000 in 10 Years
[1] Joshua Project, accessed September 26, 2018, https://joshuaproject.net/.

[2] As quoted on Joshua Project, "What Is a People Group," accessed September 26, 2018, https://joshuaproject.net/resources/articles/what_is_a_people_group.

[3] Joshua Project, Country: United States, accessed September 26, 2018, https://joshuaproject.net/countries/US.

[4] John S. Dickerson, *The Great Evangelical Recession: 6 Factors That Will Crash the American Church . . . and How to Prepare* (Grand Rapids, MI: Baker Books, 2013), 26.

5 David Garrison, *Church Planting Movements: How God Is Redeeming a Lost World* (Midlothian, VA: WIGTake Resources, 2004), 40.

6 Garrison, 89.

7 Garrison, 279.

8 Garrison, 279.

Chapter 3: The Whiteboard

1 David Barrett and Todd Johnson, *World Christian Trends* (Pasadena, CA: William Carey Library, 2001), 841.

2 Roy Moran, *Spent Matches* (Nashville: Thomas Nelson, 2015), 10–11.

3 John S. Dickerson, *The Great Evangelical Recession: 6 Factors That Will Crash the American Church . . . and How to Prepare* (Grand Rapids, MI: Baker Books, 2013).

4 Dickerson, 22.

5 Dickerson, 88, 128.

6 Dickerson, 189.

7 ExperienceLifeNow.com, "Meltdown" sermon series, http://experiencelifenow.com/series/meltdown/.

8 Dickerson, 27.

9 Christine Wicker, *The Fall of the Evangelical Nation: The Surprising Crisis Inside the Church* (New York: HarperCollins, 2008), ix.

Chapter 4: Millions

1 David Barrett and Todd Johnson, *World Christian Trends* (Pasadena, CA: William Carey Library, 2001), 841.

2 Brother Yun and Paul Hattaway, *The Heavenly Man: The Remarkable True Story of Christian Brother Yun* (London; Grand Rapids, MI: Monarch Books, 2002), 7.

3 Yun and Hattaway, 7.

4 John S. Dickerson, *The Great Evangelical Recession: 6 Factors That Will Crash the American Church . . . and How to Prepare* (Grand Rapids, MI: Baker Books, 2013).

5 Roy Moran, *Spent Matches* (Nashville: Thomas Nelson, 2015).

6 David Garrison, *Church Planting Movements: How God Is Redeeming a Lost World* (Midlothian, VA: WIGTake Resources, 2004).

Chapter 5: What Is DMM?

[1] Jerry Trousdale, *Miraculous Movements: How Hundreds of Thousands of Muslims Are Falling in Love with Jesus* (Nashville: Thomas Nelson, 2012).

[2] Jerry Trousdale and Glenn Sunshine, *The Kingdom Unleashed* (Nashville: DMM Library, 2018).

[3] Roy Moran, *Spent Matches* (Nashville: Thomas Nelson, 2015).

[4] David Garrison, *Church Planting Movements: How God Is Redeeming a Lost World* (Midlothian, VA: WIGTake Resources, 2004).

[5] David Watson and Paul Watson, *Contagious Disciple Making: Leading Others on a Journey of Discovery* (Nashville: Thomas Nelson, 2014).

[6] Garrison, 28.

[7] Moran, 109.

[8] Trousdale, *Miraculous Movements*, 16.

[9] I had a conversation about this with David Watson in September 2018, and he encouraged me to specify a "time element" in the definition of DMM. He said he typically expects to see one hundred new churches planted among previously lost people in multiple streams to the fourth generation (sometimes beyond) by the end of forty-eight months.

[10] This comes from research done by Justin Long and the 2414 Coalition.

[11] Garrison, 196.

[12] Beyond, https://beyond.org/videos.

[13] You can find the CPM steps videos at https://vimeo.com/user20501268

Chapter 6: The Ten-Year Anniversary

[1] ExperienceLifeNow.com, "Meltdown" sermon series, http://experiencelifenow.com/series/meltdown/.

[2] John S. Dickerson, *The Great Evangelical Recession: 6 Factors That Will Crash the American Church . . . and How to Prepare* (Grand Rapids, MI: Baker Books, 2013).

[3] ExperienceLifeNow.com, "Miraculous Movements" sermon series, http://experiencelifenow.com/media/miraculous-movements/.

[4] Dana Krempels, PhD, "*Why* Spay or Neuter My Rabbit? Some Scary Numbers," January 2006, University of Miami College of Arts and Sciences, Department of Biology, http://www.bio.miami .edu/hare/scary.html.

[5] Jerry Trousdale, *Miraculous Movements: How Hundreds of Thousands of Muslims Are Falling in Love with Jesus* (Nashville: Thomas Nelson, 2012), 116.

[6] To watch the full ten-year anniversary service online, visit http:// www.wigtakedmm.com/resources.

Chapter 7: Leverage

[1] Henry and Richard Blackaby, *Experiencing God* (Nashville: B & H Publishing, 2008).

[2] "A Revival Account: Asbury 1970," Asbury College, https://www .youtube.com/watch?v=7qOqitIKUNs.

[3] Jerry Trousdale and Glenn Sunshine, *The Kingdom Unleashed* (Nashville: DMM Library, 2018), 135–36.

[4] Francis Chan, *Letters to the Church* (Colorado Springs: David C Cook, 2018), 10–15.

Chapter 9: DMM Coaching

[1] Just Coach Me Coaching Solutions, accessed September 26, 2018, http://justcoachme.org/.

[2] R. Rekedal Smith, *Dear Mom and Dad* (self-pub., CreateSpace, 2017).

Chapter 10: DMM Training

[1] For more on this couple's journey, check out their fascinating book: R. Rekedal Smith, *Dear Mom and Dad* (self-pub., CreateSpace 2017).

Chapter 12: Focus on God's Word

[1] Roy Moran, *Spent Matches* (Nashville: Thomas Nelson, 2015), 36.

[2] We did a sermon series called "Raise the Sails." The first message was on this first element. You can watch it here: http://experiencelifenow.com/video/raise-the-sails/.

Chapter 13: Multiply Extraordinary Prayer

[1] Jerry Trousdale, *Miraculous Movements: How Hundreds of Thousands of Muslims Are Falling in Love with Jesus* (Nashville: Thomas Nelson, 2012), 55–56.

[2] David Garrison, *Church Planting Movements: How God Is Redeeming a Lost World* (Midlothian, VA: WIGTake Resources, 2004), 172.

[3] Garrison, 172–73.

[4] Jim Cymbala, *Fresh Wind, Fresh Fire* (Grand Rapids, MI: Zondervan, 2008), 53, 74.

[5] Jerry Trousdale and Glenn S. Sunshine, *The Kingdom Unleashed* (Nashville: DMM Library, 2018), 67.

[6] Trousdale and Sunshine, 72–73.

[7] The second message in the "Raise the Sails" sermon series was on this second element. You can watch it here: http://experiencelifenow.com/video/raise-the-sails-part-2/.

Chapter 14: Go Out Among the Lost

[1] Steve Addison, *What Jesus Started: Joining the Movement, Changing the World* (Downers Grove, IL: IVP Books, 2012).

[2] See chapter 12, "Focus on God's Word," for the seven DBS questions.

[3] The third message in the "Raise the Sails" sermon series was on this third element. You can watch it here: http://experiencelifenow.com/video/raise-the-sails-part-3/.

Chapter 15: See Groups Start

[1] David Garrison, *Church Planting Movements: How God Is Redeeming a Lost World* (Midlothian, VA: WIGTake Resources, 2004), 21–22.

[2] The fourth message in the "Raise the Sails" sermon series was on this fourth element. You can watch it here: http://experiencelifenow.com/video/raise-the-sails-part-4/.

Chapter 16: Cast Vision

[1] Justin D. Long (@JustinDLong), "Raising up 1 team of 2 to 3 people can reach 100,000," Twitter, May 20, 2018, 6:01 p.m., https://twitter.com/justindlong/status/998368140131295232.

[2] The fifth message in the "Raise the Sails" sermon series was on this fifth element. You can watch it here: http://experiencelifenow.com/video/raise-the-sails-part-5/.

Chapter 17: Train Believers

[1] The sixth message in the "Raise the Sails" sermon series was on this sixth element. You can watch it here: http://experiencelifenow.com/video/raise-the-sails-part-6/.

Chapter 18: Ongoing Coaching

[1] Jerry Trousdale and Glenn S. Sunshine, *The Kingdom Unleashed* (Nashville: DMM Library, 2018), 13.

[2] Roy Moran, *Spent Matches* (Nashville: Thomas Nelson, 2015), 118–19.

[3] The seventh message in the "Raise the Sails" sermon series was on this seventh element. You can watch it here: http://experiencelifenow.com/video/raise-the-sails-part-7/.

Chapter 19: Akachi

[1] https://www.facebook.com/royemoran.

Chapter 20: Andrew and Kristin

[1] You can find more details about these Next Steps at http://www.experiencelifenow.com.

[2] For more information, see the Perspectives website, https://www.perspectives.org/.

[3] You can find out more about our Phase One Goer Groups at http://experiencelifenow.com/ministries/for-the-nations/.

[4] You can watch a video of Kristin sharing her story at https://vimeo.com/261356664.

Chapter 21: From Microsoft to Ministry

[1] Henry and Richard Blackaby, Claude King, *Experiencing God, Revised and Expanded ed.* (Nashville: B & H Publishing Group, 2008).

[2] Henry T. Blackaby and Richard Blackaby, *Experiencing God Day-By-Day* (Nashville: B & H Books, 1997).

Chapter 22: Seminary Elective

[1] Daniel R. Sanchez, Ebbie C. Smith, and Curtis E. Watke, *Starting Reproducing Congregations* (n.p.: ChurchStarting.net, 2001).

[2] The conference was held at Northwood Church in Keller, Texas, http://northwoodchurch.org/.

Chapter 23: From Simple to Complex

[1] Ralph W. Neighbour Jr., *Where Do We Go From Here?: A Guidebook for the Cell Group Church* (Houston, TX: Touch Publications, 2000).

[2] Joel Comiskey, *Cell Church Solutions: Transforming the Church in North America* (n.p.: CCS Publishing, 2004).

[3] Kellie Bramlet, "Experience Life Church Ranked Second Fastest Growing in the Nation," *Lubbock Avalanche-Journal*, September 21, 2010, http://www.lubbockonline.com/article/20100921/NEWS/309219772 and https://en.wikipedia.org/wiki/Experience_Life.

Chapter 24: Identity Crisis

[1] Jerry Trousdale and Glenn S. Sunshine, *The Kingdom Unleashed* (Nashville: DMM Library, 2018), 139–40.

Chapter 26: A Reduction in Attendance

[1] Jerry Trousdale, *Miraculous Movements: How Hundreds of Thousands of Muslims Are Falling in Love with Jesus* (Nashville: Thomas Nelson, 2012), 40.

[2] Jared C. Wilson (@jaredcwilson), "Pastors, you will always

discover a church's idols by changing things," Twitter, June 21, 2018, 6:44 a.m., https://twitter.com/jaredcwilson/status/1009794068468117504. Jared is an author and director of Content Strategy for Midwestern Baptist Theological Seminary.

Chapter 27: Doubts and Discouragement

[1] Jerry Trousdale and Glenn S. Sunshine, *The Kingdom Unleashed* (Nashville: Thomas Nelson, 2018), 345.

Chapter 29: Poor

[1] You can find the CPM steps videos at https://vimeo.com /user20501268.

Chapter 30: International

[1] For more information, see the Perspectives website, https://www .perspectives.org/.

[2] For more information about Launch Global, see their website, http://www.launchglobal.org/.

[3] You can find out more about our Phase One Goer Groups at http:// experiencelifenow.com/ministries/for-the-nations/.

[4] See appendix 2 for the Creation to Christ sequence.

Chapter 31: Prisoner

[1] John Giuffo, "America's Most Dangerous Cities 2011," *Forbes* magazine, October 3, 2011, https:// www.forbes.com/sites/johngiuffo/2011/10/03 /americas-most-dangerous-cities/#5d7b45d576bd.

[2] See "#6 Lubbock, Texas" in *Forbes* magazine's photo gallery of America's most dangerous cities, https://www.forbes.com /pictures/efel45mde/6-lubbock-texas/#23da8f5c2fd0.

[3] ExperienceLifeNow.com, "Freedom Campus—LCDC," http://experiencelifenow.com/locations/freedom-campus-lcdc/.

Chapter 32: Sick

[1] Jerry Trousdale and Glenn S. Sunshine, *The Kingdom Unleashed* (Nashville: DMM Library, 2018), 226.

[2] David Garrison, *Church Planting Movements: How God Is Redeeming a Lost World* (Midlothian, VA: WIGTake Resources, 2004), 232–33.

[3] You can find the CPM steps videos at https://vimeo.com /user20501268.

Chapter 33: Tentmaking

[1] See chapter 6 for more information on rabbit churches and chapters 22 and 23 for more information on simple churches. I'm using those terms synonymously.

Chapter 34: Weekend Planning

[1] Jerry Trousdale, *Miraculous Movements: How Hundreds of Thousands of Muslims Are Falling in Love with Jesus* (Nashville: Thomas Nelson, 2012), 100.

Chapter 38: How to Get Started (Church Staff)

[1] John S. Dickerson, *The Great Evangelical Recession: 6 Factors That Will Crash the American Church . . . and How to Prepare* (Grand Rapids, MI: Baker Books, 2013).

[2] Jerry Trousdale, *Miraculous Movements: How Hundreds of Thousands of Muslims Are Falling in Love with Jesus* (Nashville: Thomas Nelson, 2012).

[3] Roy Moran, *Spent Matches* (Nashville: Thomas Nelson, 2015).

[4] David Garrison, *Church Planting Movements: How God Is Redeeming a Lost World* (Midlothian, VA: WIGTake Resources, 2004).

[5] Jerry Trousdale and Glenn S. Sunshine, *The Kingdom Unleashed* (Nashville: DMM Library, 2018).

[6] wigtakedmm.com, http://wigtakedmm.com/resources/.

[7] Contact us at info@wigtakedmm.com.

8 ExperienceLifeNow.com, "Meltdown" sermon series, http://experiencelifenow.com/series/meltdown/.

9 ExperienceLifeNow.com, "Miraculous Movements" sermon series, http://experiencelifenow.com/media/miraculous-movements/.

Chapter 39: How to Get Started (Church Attendees)

1 Email us at info@wigtakedmm.com.

2 wigtakedmm.com, http://www.wigtakedmm.com/resources.

Chapter 40: Can This *Really* Happen in America?

1 For more information about Cityteam, see their website, https://www.cityteam.org/.

2 This is quoted from an email Hermie sent to me explaining this.

3 Roy Moran, *Spent Matches* (Nashville: Thomas Nelson, 2015), 24.

4 David Garrison, *Church Planting Movements: How God Is Redeeming a Lost World* (Midlothian, VA: WIGTake Resources, 2004), 277–78.

5 John S. Dickerson, *The Great Evangelical Recession: 6 Factors That Will Crash the American Church . . . and How to Prepare* (Grand Rapids, MI: Baker Books, 2013), 32.